The Plays of HENRY FIELDING:
A Critical Study of His Dramatic Career

The Plays of Henry Fielding:
A Critical Study of His
Dramatic Career

ALBERT J. RIVERO

UNIVERSITY PRESS OF VIRGINIA
CHARLOTTESVILLE

The University Press of Virginia
Copyright © 1989 by the Rector and Visitors
of the University of Virginia

First published 1989

Library of Congress Cataloging-in-Publication Data

Rivero, Albert J., 1953–
    The plays of Henry Fielding : a critical study of his
dramatic career / Albert J. Rivero.
        p.   cm.
    Includes index.
    ISBN 0-8139-1228-8
    1. Fielding, Henry, 1707–1754—Dramatic works. 2. Theater—
England—London—History—18th century. I. Title.
    PR3548.D7R58 1989
882'.5—dc 19   88-35304
                                                                         CIP

Printed in the United States of America

For my mother and in memory of my father

Contents

Preface

THE PLAYS OF HENRY FIELDING, while far from being neglected, have not received the critical attention they deserve. As Robert D. Hume has observed, "Few scholars have been much interested in Fielding's highly successful career as a dramatist. To most it has seemed a false start. Readers tend to find the conventional plays derivative and sentimental, the topical ones scrappy and superficial."[1] Thus, although the list of articles, dissertations, and chapters of books devoted to the plays is relatively long—Hume's reference to "few scholars" is somewhat misleading—and includes the works of such distinguished scholars as Sheridan Baker, J. Paul Hunter, Ronald Paulson, E. V. Roberts, and C. B. Woods, until the spring of 1988, only one book had ever been published on the subject: Ducrocq's *Le théâtre de Fielding, 1728–1737, et ses prolongements dans l'oeuvre romanesque.*[2] Admirably researched and—in Pat Rogers's word—"workmanlike" in its exposition,[3] Ducrocq's study nonetheless evinces, as its title suggests, what has been the most pervasive critical assumption underlying the evaluation of the plays: namely, that these early dramatic pieces merit attention only insofar as they serve as prologue to the later fiction.[4] In this view Fielding from the very beginning of his career wanted to write novels but somehow did not heed his true calling until after 1737, when the Licensing Act providentially ended his often not so harmless drudgery as a theatrical hack.

The teleological fallacy on which this view is based has prevented critics from examining these early works in their own right, as dramatic entities worthy of serious critical scrutiny. To seek adumbrations of the older master of prose fiction in the younger apprentice of the theater is to ignore Fielding's considerable accomplishment and technical daring as a playwright. Fielding was not exhausting the possibilities of the theater, but trying to expand them; he was not, in other words, writing plays with novelistic features. Instead, he came to see that the five-act, well-made play of the Restoration and early eighteenth century had reached a dead end, both in subject matter and in method. The social, political, and aesthetic realities of the 1730s demanded new approaches, new forms, new emphases. Fielding set out to discover new ways of constructing plays.

What is needed is a new approach to Fielding's dramatic career. Such an approach is precisely what Robert D. Hume offers in *Henry Fielding and the London Theatre.*[5] Although Hume's book has appeared too late to guide my research and writing I am glad to see that Hume, approaching Fielding's dramatic career from the perspective of the theater historian, arrives at an estimate similar to mine. Yet Hume's book, primarily a historical survey of Fielding's involvement with the theater, is not in any sense a critical analysis of the plays, which are treated fairly briefly one by one in the context of dramatic and theatrical events in London in the 1730s. Hume's book is now the principal authority for the facts of Fielding's theatrical career, and I shall refer to it in my text and notes whenever reference to those facts is necessary to my argument. My study complements Hume's in offering a critical—rather than biographical and historical—account of Fielding's dramatic career.

It has often been observed that a book is never finished but abandoned at a convenient point. This observation holds true here. This small book offers one version, one story of Fielding's dramatic career; other stories could be written by choosing other examples, other plays, by plotting the action along other points of reference. But the writer, either of fictions or of criticism, must choose from among possibilities and relations, and create, in Henry James's memorable phrase, a geometry of his own. My geometry is, inevitably, of my own making but true, I hope, to the facts of Fielding's life in the theater. It is my wish that my efforts will encourage others to pick up the story where I have left off, amend it, or fashion their own versions to challenge mine.

My purpose in the pages that follow, then, is to tell my story of Fielding's dramatic career. This modest aim has guided my approach and method. Since I believe that the best way to tell the

story of Fielding's dramatic career is to focus on the plays themselves, I offer detailed critical readings of ten representative plays.
Some unsympathetic readers might, of course, view these detailed
analyses as just descriptions of obscure works. But the charge of
obscurity—given the published evidence, few critics, even special-
ists in eighteenth-century drama, are acquainted with the plays—
provides, in this respect, a most compelling argument for what
might appear to be, at first glance, an unnecessary devotion to textual matters. Writing in *The Clark Newsletter,* Simon Varey accurately captures what has thus far been the dominant attitude
toward early eighteenth-century British theater and Fielding's role
in it: "The foremost dramatist of the day . . . was . . . Colley Cibber, whose reputation has been entirely submerged by Pope's ele-
vating him to the exalted position of Arch Dunce. Since the plays
of Cibber's only serious rival, Henry Fielding, are hardly even read
these days, let alone performed, the earlier eighteenth-century theater tends to be passed over with (at best) a polite cough."[6]

There is another reason for offering detailed analysis. Of
Fielding's twenty-six plays, only five—all of them irregular—have
been published in modern critical editions. The regular comedies,
available only in Henley's 1902 edition of the collected works, are
virtually unknown: they are usually dismissed in favor of the more
"interesting" and "vital" irregular satires or praised in terms so general and vague as to suggest that the critic knows little about them.
In short, while someone writing on *The Country Wife* or *The Man of
Mode* can safely assume that his reader will be acquainted with its
plot, characters, and themes, someone writing on *Love in Several
Masques, The Temple Beau,* or even *The Modern Husband* cannot make
such an assumption. The most basic mode of descriptive criticism
is needed to rectify the present imbalance in our evaluation of
Fielding's career as a playwright. Once we have taken this initial
step, we shall be in a position to move on to subtler forms of critical
scrutiny and discrimination. Moreover, I would argue that such
critical descriptions are needed to establish what these plays are
about, to explore their themes, to appreciate Fielding's dramatic
techniques, to examine his way of constructing plays—in short, to
determine the shape of his dramatic career.

And I have chosen, finally, to tell the story of that dramatic career without burdening the reader with an exhaustive history of contemporary plays and playwrights. Instead, I sketch out the historical context for Fielding's dramatic career in terms of trends in contemporary dramatic affairs that help to account for his artistic choices in individual plays. The plays themselves serve as the focus of my story from beginning to end. It is not my intention, at this point, to write a history of British drama from 1728 to 1737, or to trace in detail the filiations of Fielding's dramatic works, but rather to offer a critical study of his dramatic career through the examination of ten plays which, in my view, mark significant moments in his theatrical life.[7]

I have incurred many debts in the writing of this book. First and foremost, I wish to thank Martin C. Battestin, who encouraged me to begin this project and, with kindness and patience, supervised its progress. His careful reading of the several versions of this study has saved me from many inaccuracies, factual, argumentative, and stylistic; all the flaws that remain are, I fear, my own. Ralph Cohen and the late Irvin Ehrenpreis not only wrote innumerable letters in support of this project, but also generously contributed their time and knowledge at crucial points in its development. Robert D. Hume offered words of encouragement at a time when it appeared, at least to me, that the project was no longer worth pursuing. Lisa M. Furrey proofread several drafts, and, whenever needed, gave generously of her wisdom and love. The staff of the University Press of Virginia, especially the late Walker Cowen, have been most helpful.

Several institutions and individuals at those institutions also deserve my thanks. A Summer Faculty Grant from Marquette University in 1983 allowed me to travel to Great Britain, to examine documents at the British Library, the Bodleian, the Cambridge University Library, the University of Edinburgh Library, and the National Library of Scotland. James E. Swearingen, my chairman, arranged a year-long leave of absence in 1985, during which I was able to complete most of my research and writing. Financial support for that year was provided by a Research Fellowship for Recent Recipients of the Ph.D. from the American Council of Learned Societies (with the contribution of the National Endowment for the Humanities) and an Exxon Education Foundation Fellowship from the Newberry Library in Chicago, where I spent six months in pleasant surroundings and even more pleasant company; Richard Brown and Paul Gehl of the Newberry merit special mention for their interest in and support of my work. Although illness prevented me from accepting its bounty, I am grateful to the Fellowship Committee of the Clark Library, UCLA, for awarding me a Summer Postdoctoral Fellowship in 1986.

Finally, I thank the editor of *Restoration and Eighteenth-Century Theatre Research* for permission to use, in chapter 2, material that first appeared in the Winter 1986 issue of that journal under the title "Fielding's Artistic Accommodations in *The Author's Farce* (1730)."

The Plays of HENRY FIELDING:
A Critical Study of His Dramatic Career

There are your acting plays and your reading plays. . . . Your acting play is entirely supported by the merit of the actor, without any regard to the author at all. In this case, it signifies very little whether there be any sense in it or no. Now your reading play is of a different stamp and must have wit and meaning in it. These latter I call your substantive, as being able to support themselves. The former are your adjective, as what require the buffoonery and gestures of an actor to be joined to them to show their signification.

—Bookweight, in *The Author's Farce*

The whole odiousness of the thing lies in the connection between drama and theatre. The one is admirable in its interest and difficulty, the other loathsome in its conditions. If the drama could only be theoretically or hypothetically acted, the fascination resident in its all but unconquerable (*circumspice!*) form would be unimpaired and one would be able to have the exquisite exercise without the horrid sacrifice.

—Henry James

Introduction

Eighty years ago George Bernard Shaw called Fielding "the greatest practising dramatist, with the single exception of Shakespeare, produced by England between the Middle Ages and the nineteenth century."[1] Even the most ardent admirer of Fielding's plays must admit that this estimate—to quote the words of a scholar who devoted most of his life to their study—"seems somewhat rash."[2] No amount of critical pleading can convince me, for instance, that Fielding is a better dramatist than, say, Jonson, Dryden, Wycherley, Congreve, or Gay. To put it simply, not one of Fielding's plays, taken on its own merits, can rival the best work of these eminent men of the theater. *Bartholomew Fair*, *The Conquest of Granada*, *The Country Wife*, *The Way of the World*, and *The Beggar's Opera* are classics of our literature; *The Author's Farce*, *Tom Thumb*, *The Modern Husband*, *Pasquin*, and *The Historical Register* are not.

Yet there is a sense in which Shaw's words convey some truth. Fielding may not have been "the greatest practising dramatist" in the English tradition, the keeper of the flame during the long dark night between Shakespeare and Shaw, but he was certainly one of the most interesting playwrights because of his historical position, similar to that of Shaw himself, and his awareness of what it meant to be a playwright at a time when the native dramatic tradition appeared to have settled down for a long sleep and the only hope for an awakening lay in such low crowd-pleasers as farces, puppet shows, "laughing" tragedies, and ballad operas. Fortunately for Fielding, Gay had jolted the town in 1728 and given his most able disciple a glimpse of an exciting theatrical future. That future, with all its bright promises, lasted less than ten years. Politics, the unavoidable subject matter of a playwright writing in Walpole's England, proved Fielding's undoing. And Fielding's political satire

I

was no doubt what appealed most to Shaw and the main reason for his rash estimate. Unlike Colley Cibber, who vilified Fielding—for "set[ting] Fire to his Stage, by writing up to an Act of Parliament to demolish it"—Shaw admired the courage and wit of the "*Herculean* Satyrist . . . that seem'd to knock all Distinctions of Mankind on the Head."[3] Shaw, the self-appointed censor and debunker of his age, regarded Fielding as a kindred spirit, as a man who understood that the playwright ought to be the legislator, unacknowledged or otherwise, of the world.

Shaw, I suggest, also admired Fielding for a more purely literary or theatrical reason, though I doubt that Shaw would have granted that one can divorce literature from politics and speak of literary technique as separate from political commitment. For if Fielding was not the greatest dramatist between Shakespeare and Shaw, he was unquestionably one of the most innovative, unafraid to experiment with dramatic forms, from the most conventional to the most improbable. Fielding did not hesitate to break old dramatic laws and create new ones as he pleased; he was the acknowledged legislator of his own theatrical world. It is in this sense that I begin to agree with Shaw's hyperbolic assessment of Fielding's dramatic achievement, and I shall try, in the following pages, to present a case for the significance of his dramatic career. But that significance, as I shall argue throughout this study, cannot be fully appreciated until we stop considering his work in the theater as prologue to the future novels.[4] The most innovative and popular English playwright of the 1730s deserves a better fate.

The dismissal of Fielding's plays as apprentice work for the novels stems from a curious misreading of literary evidence, and in this respect it has wide implications for the writing and understanding of literary history. While it is true that the drama declined and the novel rose in the early eighteenth century, it is perilous to infer a causal connection between these two events. Cross-genre critics delight in pointing out how certain elements that could no longer be comfortably housed in dramatic forms end up in the more hospitable surroundings of the novel; Fielding's switch from drama to prose fiction is usually adduced as the clincher for this hypothesis.[5] Yet a careful study of Fielding's dramatic career reveals that playwrights in the 1720s and 1730s were keenly aware that the traditional plots and techniques of regular comedy and heroic trag-edy had run their course. Rather than becoming novelists, these playwrights sought other themes, other ways of constructing plays. As the most perceptive and far-sighted of early eighteenth-century playwrights, Fielding sensed that the future of the theater lay in irregular drama like Gay's and in drama of serious social commen-tary like Lillo's.[6] The Licensing Act of 1737 ended Fielding's exper-iments in irregular forms and led him to explore his serious social concerns in prose fiction because the theater was, by law, closed to him; legal coercion and economic necessity can provide a most per-suasive argument for altering one's mode of literary expression.

We can consider the drama as a declining genre, then, only from the outside, from the vantage point of historical hindsight; from the inside, from an analysis of individual plays and of individ-ual dramatic careers, we can begin to appreciate the decade before the Licensing Act as one of the most exciting and vital in the his-tory of the English theater as dramatists devoted their energies to expanding the thematic and formal possibilities of their chosen me-dium. In short, the history of early eighteenth-century English the-ater—particularly of the decade between *The Beggar's Opera* and the Licensing Act—needs to be written from a new perspective. And in writing this new history, we must allow irregular drama to play its rightful prominent role.[7] Fielding stands at the center of this dramatic development; this is why a study of his career as a play-wright is so instructive.

Fielding began his dramatic career with a bow to the tradition. His first two plays, *Love in Several Masques* (1728) and *The Temple Beau* (1730), which I examine in my opening chapter, show him already in command of the techniques of regular comedy. While derivative, these two plays are no mere pastiches of Congreve, Steele, and Cibber but masterly appropriations of traditional material. In their concern with defining the merits of the good man and woman in the context of marriage, these plays also announce the serious social commentator. For Fielding, tradition and the individual talent in-tersected at a moral center.

The initial rejection of *The Temple Beau*, however, convinced Fielding that his future success would depend on his ability to satisfy the town's taste for less conventional entertainments. As Witmore advises Harry Luckless in *The Author's Farce* (1730), "If you must write, write nonsense, write operas, write entertainments, write *Hurlothrumbos*, set up an *Oratory* and preach nonsense, and you may meet with encouragement enough."[8] Audiences nurtured on French pantomimes, harlequinades, and Italian operas could not be expected to relish the meaning and wit of regular comedy. The town demanded spectacle, "acting" rather than "reading" plays. Following the examples of Molière and Gay, Fielding began to write acting plays with wit and meaning in them. My second, third, and fifth chapters demonstrate how Fielding found his own distinctive voice by parodying the pleasures of the town. These chapters offer detailed analyses of the language and satiric strategies of *The Author's Farce*, the *Tom Thumb* plays (1730; 1731), and the several versions of *The Grub-Street Opera* (1731). In Fielding's hands these provisional, parodic forms, meant to clear the stage of the debris of inept hacks and thus prepare the way for more rational productions, became compelling theater.

But Fielding did not wish to relinquish regular dramatic forms. His aim was to revitalize traditional drama by eliminating its clichés and outmoded conventions, not to ensure its demise. In my fourth chapter I examine *Rape upon Rape* (1730), a play which, while exhibiting many features of regular drama, shows Fielding's use of the theater to address specific social issues. Taking as its point of reference the recent pardon of the infamous Colonel Charteris, the play wittily exposes the flaws in a legal system that lets a convicted rapist go free. The iniquities encouraged by unequal laws are also the topic explored in *The Modern Husband* (1732), the subject of my sixth chapter. This solemn play deals with the practice, encouraged by the Criminal Conduct laws, of selling one's wife for personal interest. In its unflinching depiction of ugly social fact, *The Modern Husband* anticipates Ibsen. Free of the wit traps and stylization of conventional comedy, the play, though it achieved a respectable run of fourteen performances, was not warmly received by its original audience; its opening night was disrupted by hissing and it was never revived. Its serious purpose and design could only be wasted on a public eager for spectacular nonsense.

4

Introduction

After the less than enthusiastic reception of *The Modern Husband*, Fielding seems to have given up on regular comedy; his other exercises in the genre are perfunctory at best, though his subsequent imitations of Molière suggest that while he may have decided not to attempt another original regular comedy, he could still preserve the old forms in adaptations of proven models. Perhaps he was biding his time until he could try again; we shall never know. What we do know is that the Drury Lane actors' strike of 1733, coupled with his newfound commitment to the Opposition signaled by the dedication of *Don Quixote in England* (1734) to Lord Chesterfield, caused Fielding to return to irregular forms with renewed vigor, to explore the many nuances and complexities of the state-stage metaphor.[9] *Pasquin* (1736) and *The Historical Register for the Year 1736* (1737) show Fielding at the height of his dramatic powers. My last chapter deals with how the politics of the playhouse determined the structure and techniques of his last two satirical plays. At this point the Licensing Act intervened; the rest, except for revivals and Garrick's staging of three unacted comedies from the early 1730s, is silence.

CHAPTER I

A Bow to the Tradition:
Love in Several Masques and
The Temple Beau

HAD FIELDING WISHED to underscore his kinship to his dramatic precursors in a striking fashion, he could not have chosen a better setting for the initial performance of *Love in Several
Masques*. The play opened at the Theatre Royal, Drury Lane, on
16 February 1728.[1] Here, on the same stage that had witnessed the
triumphs of the most eminent dramatists and actors of the Restoration and the first decades of the eighteenth century, Fielding had
the pleasure of seeing his first theatrical effort. The play followed
The Provok'd Husband, Colley Cibber's highly successful adaptation
and completion of *A Journey to London*, a series of dramatic sketches
left unfinished by Sir John Vanbrugh at his death in 1726. Fielding's cast included several of the most distinguished actors of the
day: Cibber as Rattle, Mills as Wisemore, Wilks as Merital, and
Mrs. Oldfield as Lady Matchless. As the nucleus of the Drury
Lane company, these four talented performers had often acted together, most notably six years before, as members of the original
cast of *The Conscious Lovers*. They had earned fame and fortune by
appearing in many of those very plays, both old and new, on which
Fielding had modeled his own. *Love in Several Masques*, in short,
appeared in a milieu redolent with theatrical tradition. Moreover,
it managed to achieve a respectable run of four nights, despite its
having to compete with that most popular and influential of
eighteenth-century plays, Gay's *Beggar's Opera*. All things considered, it was a most auspicious beginning for the aspiring playwright.

The preface to the play reveals that from the beginning Fielding was a writer deeply conscious of the literary past and of his relation to it. This consciousness of the past is, of course, not unusual in an eighteenth-century author, nor is the writing of prefaces to express that consciousness remarkable. But, viewed from the perspective of Fielding's whole career, this preface looks forward to all those documents—particularly the preface to *Joseph Andrews* and several of the introductory chapters to *Tom Jones*—in which Fielding defines his work in terms of the work of his predecessors and contemporaries. I quote the first two paragraphs of the preface to *Love in Several Masques:*

> I believe few plays have ever adventured into the world under greater disadvantages than this. First, as it succeeded a comedy which, for the continued space of twenty-eight nights, received as great (and as just) applauses, as ever were bestowed on the English Theatre. And secondly, as it is co-temporary with an entertainment which engrosses the whole talk and admiration of the town.
>
> These were difficulties which seemed rather to require the superior force of a Wycherley, or a Congreve, than of a raw and unexperienced pen; for I believe I may boast that none ever appeared so early upon the stage. However, such was the candour of the audience, the play was received with greater satisfaction than I should have promised myself from its merit, had it even preceded the Provoked Husband.[2]

The tone here is both diffident and defiant. Fielding bows gracefully in the direction of his two dramatic contemporaries, Cibber and Gay, indicating that he is succeeding one (Cibber) while competing against the other (Gay). In addition, he makes a generic distinction between their works: *The Provok'd Husband* is a "comedy"; *The Beggar's Opera*, an "entertainment." *Love in Several Masques* follows *The Provok'd Husband* not only chronologically but generically; it belongs to a tradition of comedy that though once the reigning diversion of the town, now finds itself in competition with entertainments. Fielding thus places the historical event of his first appearance on the London stage within the larger context of contemporary theatrical affairs and transforms it into an emblem of the situation faced by new playwrights who as they venture into the theater world of 1728 must choose between regular comedy and irregular entertainments. Fielding initially aligns himself with Cibber, the latest writer of comedy, against Gay, the latest writer of entertainments.

But this initial alignment with Cibber is subverted almost immediately as Fielding reveals that even though his play followed Cibber's, he regards the popularity of *The Provok'd Husband* as another one of the "disadvantages" or "difficulties" that *Love in Several Masques* had to overcome. Indeed, by the end of the second paragraph Fielding almost manages, in a conditional clause, to alter the chronology of events. The reception of *Love in Several Masques*, Fielding suggests, would have been the same even if it had "preceded the Provoked Husband." Given the historical record, Fielding's wish for precedence could remain only a rhetorical move, his compliment to "the candour of the audience" masking his recognition that while Gay provided the actual competition to *Love in Several Masques*, there was an even greater threat to regular comedy in general—and Henry Fielding in particular—from an enemy within.

Fielding's desire to get behind Cibber, to connect himself with the tradition of dramatic comedy without having to follow its latest practitioner, finds expression in his invocation of Wycherley and Congreve. As author, player, and manager (with Booth and Wilks) of Drury Lane, Cibber was the living link to the tradition Fielding wished to join; Wycherley had died in 1715, and Congreve, though still alive, had not written a play since *The Way of the World* (1700). But Fielding, for reasons he perhaps did not yet fully understand or did not wish to spell out—they would be revealed later, in the preface to *Plutus* (1742), for example, and *Tom Jones* (12.5)—follows the acknowledgment of his succession from Cibber with the discovery of the old masters whose "superior force" he must possess in order to succeed against both Cibberian comedy and "cotemporary" entertainments. He might not yet be another Wycherley or another Congreve—though the moderate success of his "raw and unexperienced pen" is encouraging—but he knows who his true models must be. *The Provok'd Husband* might have "received as great (and as just) applauses"—the parentheses make this praise grudging at best—"as ever were bestowed on the English Theatre," but Fielding would rather follow Cibber's models than Cibber him-

Burden of the past

8

self. As the preface draws to its conclusion, Fielding acknowledges that he is "grateful" to Cibber, but only in his role as one of the "performers." Like Cibber's notorious address to the reader of *The Provok'd Husband*, Fielding's preface ends with a tribute to the "ravishing perfections" of Mrs. Oldfield.

The preface to *Love in Several Masques* reveals, then, not only Fielding's attempt to establish his relation to the dramatic past and present but also his reservations and anxieties about his unavoidable association with Colley Cibber. Fielding recognizes that to have his plays acted at Drury Lane, he must have the approval of his famous contemporary. To gain that approval, Fielding must follow Cibber—if not write like him, certainly write plays that he will like. The beginning of Fielding's lifelong difficulties with Cibber can thus be traced to their first theatrical collaboration. Cibber could make or break Fielding's dramatic career. Although he had agreed to stage *Love in Several Masques*—perhaps because of the good offices of Fielding's cousin, Lady Mary Wortley Montagu, to whom the play was dedicated—he could refuse or alter any future play submitted by the young dramatist, as he had done over and over with the work of other playwrights.[3] Indeed, Cibber's "Sir, it will not do" was legendary. For example, the author of *The Laureat: or, The Right Side of Colley Cibber, Esq.* (1740) sketches the following "rejection" scene:

> A certain young Gentleman, who had written a Play, applied to you as Corrector of *Drury-Lane* House, to look over his Piece, and see if you thought it fit for Representation. He had not a full-bottom'd Periwig to recommend him, and perhaps his Cloaths might be but plain and worn:—He knock'd at your Door, and gave into your Hand a Roll of Paper as he stood on the Threshold, the Door being but half open'd, and desired you would read it, and give him your Opinion: You turn'd over the first Leaf, and having read only two Lines, you returned it, with these Words, *Sir, it will not do.*[4]

While understandable in the context of his role as manager of Drury Lane, Cibber's refusal of new plays was seen by many contemporary critics as one of the principal causes contributing to the decay of the English dramatic tradition. Dennis, writing in 1725, trenchantly observed:

9

The partiality of the Town makes the Managers of the Theatre in Drury Lane stick to their old Plays, and reject all new ones un- lesse those which are forcd upon them. For either a new play succeeds or it does not. If it does not succeed, They are sure to have several Thin Houses, of which the other Theatre does not fail to make their Advantage. If it does succeed the whole profits of Three or Four nights goe away to the Author. Soe that They are sure to Thrive by their Indolence, and never fail to loose by their Industry. From hence comes their mortal aversion to new plays, and from hence their Insolent Treatment of those who write them that those who have Genius may be as much Dis- couraged from such attempts. Tis true at this rate the English Drama is like to be lost, to the Disreputation of England, and the opprobrium of those who support them.[5]

Dennis's assessment of "the causes of the decay and defects of dra- matick poetry, and of the degeneracy of the publick tast"—to quote the second title he gave to this unpublished piece written in reply to Welsted's preface to *Epistles, Odes, &c.* (1724)—is long and de- tailed and, as usual with Dennis, an invigorating mixture of Aris- totelian doctrine, common sense, contempt for foreign influences, and personal invective. Dennis blames the town for its "partiality," but the villain of the piece is Cibber. He is not a gentleman, like the managers of old; he is an inept playwright, an "Amphibious creature, Half Player, Half Poetaster, like that Leathern wingd an- imal, that takes its groveling flight in the Dusk, and passes for a singing Bird only with Beasts, and for a Beast with all the Tunefull choir."[6] In the prophetic language with which Dennis concludes his opening paragraph, Cibber is an antitype to the "Charming Choir" of "Milton, Denham, Waller, Cowley, Butler, Dryden, Rochester, Dorsett, Otway, Wycherly, Etherege, Shadwell, &c." who "flourished" in the "Reign of King Charles the second," a choir that includes "Two Comick poets" (Congreve and Vanbrugh) from the "Reign of King William," even though by then "things [had begun] apace to Degenerate."[7] Given the current state of poetic affairs in general and Cibber's influence on dramatic poetry in par- ticular, Dennis advances—in anticipation of Pope's prophetic vi- sion at the end of the last version of *The Dunciad* (1743) of a degenerate world presided over by the "Doge of Drury Lane"— that "we may without the spirit of prophesie foresee that the condition of the British Parnassus will be in a little time and be in a great measure the very same that Isaiah foretold would be the state of Babylon Immediately after its fall."[8]

I have quoted generously from Dennis's essay on the sad state of English drama in the 1720s because whatever its inaccuracies and intemperance in tone, it is representative of a commonly held view. It was almost a universally accepted proposition that contemporary dramatists were inferior to their predecessors, that Colley Cibber—to cite everyone's favorite example—represented a falling off from Wycherley, Congreve, or any other playwright of the past. While Dryden could boast, in *An Essay of Dramatick Poesie* (1668), that contemporary dramatists had improved on the tradition of Jonson and Shakespeare and could "prophecy," in his prefatory poem to *The Double-Dealer* (1694), that Congreve, his worthy descendant, would one day sit "High on the Throne of Wit," Dennis could only "prophesie" decay and degeneracy. While Dennis, in June of 1695, could hail Congreve, "after Mr. *Wicherly*," as "incomparably the best Writer of [comedy] living,"[9] thirty years later all he could do was to look back and note that after Wycherley and Congreve the poetic laurels had become a dunce's cap to be worn by the likes of Steele and Cibber. No wonder, then, that the young Fielding longed for "the superior force of a Wycherley, or a Congreve." If the tradition of comedy was to survive—and thus compete successfully against "co-temporary" entertainments—it had to be revitalized by a return to its originals. Cibber was a bad copy of those originals—a squawking bird to that "Tunefull choir"—whose "genteel" comedies, as Fielding would explain several years later, were neither funny nor well written, the "pretty, dapper, brisk, smart, pert Dialogue . . . first introduced with infinite Wit by *Wycherley* [having] at last degenerated into [the] sort of Pleasantry" found in *The Provok'd Husband*.[10]

It was indeed the controversy surrounding the production of *The Provok'd Husband* that had once more focused public attention on the many inadequacies—real or imagined—of Colley Cibber and, in particular, on his contributions to the decay of English comic drama. Many contemporaries suspected that in completing Vanbrugh's play, Cibber had managed to exact his final revenge on the man who had ridiculed, in *The Relapse; or, Virtue in Danger* (No-

vember 1696), the improbability of the ending of *Love's Last Shift*
(January 1696). Vanbrugh had demonstrated that Cibber's depiction of a virtuous wife's last-act reclamation of her rakish husband
was sentimental twaddle, an effective theatrical moment perhaps,
but not true to human nature. In *The Provok'd Wife* (1677) Vanbrugh
had continued to explore the woes of unhappy married life. Like
Mrs. Sullen in Farquhar's *The Beaux Stratagem* (1707), Vanbrugh's
Lady Brute is married to a drunkard; unlike Mrs. Sullen, who is
released from her bondage in a fairy-tale "divorce" ending, Lady
Brute cannot escape the beastly treatment of Sir John Brute. Cibber's *The Careless Husband* (1704)—which features the part of Lord
Foppington from *The Relapse*, once again acted by Cibber—had carried marital reconciliation to new heights, nowhere more so than in
the celebrated "Steinkirk" scene (5.5). The result of this dramatic
exchange was the identification in the public mind of each playwright with a certain kind of comic outlook. Cibber was seen as
"soft," the purveyor of fine sentiment and improbable happy endings; Vanbrugh was seen as "hard," one of the last writers in the
old Restoration mode exemplified by Wycherley in the 1670s and
carried on, with considerable allowance for changing public tastes,
particularly in *Love for Love* (1695), by Congreve in the 1690s.

Although this neat dichotomy oversimplifies the issues—
playwrights in the 1690s, as Robert D. Hume has argued, mixed
soft and hard elements in their comedies—it nonetheless reflects
the popular perception of Vanbrugh and Cibber.[11] Three days after
the first performance of *The Provok'd Husband*, for example, *Mist's
Weekly Journal* (13 January 1728) accused Cibber of having "committed . . . a most horrid, barbarous, and cruel Murder . . . upon
a posthumous Child of the late Sir John Vanbroog. . . . It was a
fine Child born, and would certainly have lived long, had it not
fallen into such cruel Hands."[12] Nonetheless, the allegedly mur-
dered dramatic offspring managed to survive the near-riot of its
opening night—when, as the Exciseman explains in *Tom Jones*, the
"Gentlemen" in the "Footman's Gallery" could not "bear" the "low
Stuff in it about a Country Gentleman come up to Town to stand
for Parliament Man"[13]—and logged over thirty performances. Cibber published his play together with Vanbrugh's fragment and
demonstrated that the "low Stuff" hissed at on the play's opening

night and omitted in subsequent performances had been Sir John's "posthumous Child." Having thus exonerated himself of the charge of cruelty to orphaned plays, Cibber goes on to reveal, in his address to the reader, that he had to change Vanbrugh's intended "Catastrophe" because the "violent Measures" of having "his Imaginary Fine Lady" turned "out of . . . Doors" by her husband, "however just they might be in real Life, were too severe for Comedy, and would want the proper Surprize, which is due to the End of a Play." Even though Cibber recognizes the improbability of his ending, if judged by the standards of real Life, he nonetheless defends his procedure on the grounds that comedy must end on a happy reversal. Moreover, as he immediately points out, "the Mitigation of her Sentence has been since justified by its Success."[14] In other words, whatever objections might be brought against the improbability of his ending, the proof of its appropriateness is that it succeeds with its audience.

Cibber's pragmatic defense of his dramatic procedures—his version of Johnson's "The Drama's Laws the Drama's Patrons give,/ For we that live to please, must please to live"[15]—is a shrewd one; it allows him to deplore the declining taste of the audience while catering to it. He admits that he is guilty as charged, but his sentence must be mitigated by the recognition that he is fully aware of what he is doing, that he knows the better course of action but must follow the worse. As he noted twelve years later, after he no longer depended on the theater for his livelihood and could thus afford to be more outspoken on the subject: "It is not to the Actor therefore, but to the vitiated and low Taste of the Spectator, that the Corruptions of the Stage (of what kind soever) have been owing. If the Publick, by whom they must live, had Spirit enough to discountenance, and declare against all the Trash and Fopperies they have been so frequently fond of, both the Actors, and the Authors, to the best of their Power, must naturally have serv'd their daily Table, with sound and wholesome Diet."[16] In 1728 he needed to be more cautious. Thus, while he acknowledges that the taste of the audience is corrupt, he does not entirely blame his spectators; instead he compliments himself for having offered them a play which proves that all is not lost: "The Favour the Town has shewn to the higher Characters in this Play, is a Proof, that their Taste is not wholly vitiated, by the barbarous Entertainments that have been so expensively set off to corrupt it: But, while the Repetition of the best old Plays is apt to give Satiety, and good new Ones are so scarce a Commodity, we must not wonder, that the poor Actors are sometimes forced to trade in Trash for a Livelihood".[17]

If Cibber's defense of his dramatic procedures in *The Provok'd Husband* was at least plausible, the document in which that defense appeared was another matter altogether. Cibber's address to the reader of his play was one of the most popular satiric butts of the next decade or so.[18] On 24 February 1728, *Mist's Weekly Journal* published a letter that set the tone for future attacks, particularly that by Fielding himself in his preface to *Tom Thumb* two years later. The author laments that he cannot "make an exact Critick upon . . . Mr. *C———r's* Preface . . . unless some Person of Learning would be so good as to translate it into *English* for me; for I own, it is written in a Language of which I understand no Part of Speech." To support this point, he offers the following mock panegyric on the word *paraphanalia*, a further distortion of Cibber's original *paraphonalia*: "There's a noble Word! Let the Admirers of *Dryden*, *Otway*, or *Wycherly*, shew me, where any of them have written so fine a Word.—The Criticks, indeed, pretend that he meant *Paraphernalia*, but that Objection will appear idle, when it can be proved, that one is as much to the Purpose as the other." This initial attack on Cibber's language serves as the prologue for a "Critick" upon *The Provok'd Husband:*

> The *Provok'd Husband* is now in Print, and those who have seen as well as read it, have had Opportunities of observing the great *Force of Action*, and of seeing how far it can improve Works of this Nature, and I venture to pronounce, that the whole Merit of this Play lies in two of the Actors, and it may teach us to account why those People [the Drury Lane managers] have endeavour'd to suppress all Writers of the least Degree of Merit; for it is probable, they may very cunningly imagine, that what is good in it self, cannot much advance the Reputation of the Actor, for there the Merit will lye in the Play; but in Things like this, the whole Praise will be the Players Right.—All which being only consider'd, it would be no impolitick Resolution in them to suffer no Person to prepare any Thing for their Stage except *C———r.*

14

The anonymous letter writer grants the success of the play but goes on to argue that that success was owing to "two Actors," not to Cibber's skills as a dramatist. Thus he insinuates that Cibber's own praise of the actors, however lavish, was actually insufficient, given his enormous debt to their talents. There is, in short, a distinction to be made between a play read in one's closet and a play acted on stage. In his preface to *Love in Several Masques*, Fielding also acknowledges this distinction between text and performance; his play could not have succeeded without "the candour of the audience" or the "advantageous" performances of its cast. This distinction between reading and acting plays, emphatically enunciated by Bookweight in *The Author's Farce*, would become, as I shall argue throughout this study, the cornerstone of Fielding's dramatic career.

Thus Cibber as manager of Drury Lane ushered Fielding into the London theater world; he also taught him, by positive and negative example, what it took to be a playwright in London in 1728. The controversy surrounding *The Provok'd Husband* had raised issues that would continue to interest and trouble Fielding; *The Beggar's Opera* seemed to offer an exciting alternative to Cibberian dramaturgy, though as Fielding soon realized, there were risks involved in being Gay's disciple. But in 1728 Cibber was the man of the theater he most needed to please.

This, then, was the immediate context of Fielding's initial theatrical adventure. *Love in Several Masques*, as befits the first effort of a young apprentice, resonates with echoes from the dramatic past. Fielding demonstrates his thorough acquaintance with his predecessors not so much by adopting specific features from their works as by creating a certain ambience. His play breathes the air of Restoration and early eighteenth-century comedy, from Etherege, Wycherley, and Congreve to Farquhar, Steele, and Cibber. At first glance the play appears to be nothing more than an unimaginative rehashing of tired Restoration patterns, a conventional five-act drama with stock characters and hackneyed situations. To a large extent *Love in Several Masques* is conventional and unimaginative, both in form and in content. The play contains virtually every feature of contemporary comic drama: wits, fools, fops, duels, references to china shops, hidings in closets, plays-within, and the like. Yet even at his most imitative Fielding manages to imprint his own unmistakable artistic personality on what he chooses to imitate. *Love in Several Masques* evinces what critics have identified as the quintessence of Fielding's art: its clear moral purpose, its conspicuous moral tone. This is not to say that earlier drama is lacking this seriousness of purpose. Restoration and eighteenth-century theater abounds in examples of explicitly moral comedies, from Shadwell's *Squire of Alsatia* (1688) to Steele's *Conscious Lovers* (1722). In this respect Fielding's moral stance imitates something already in the tradition. But by choosing this stance, Fielding announces what sort of dramatist he wishes to be, and, as it turned out, what kind of artist he would become. In addition, the play embodies those self-reflexive techniques that would continue to inform Fielding's art, both in the theater and in prose fiction. The distinctive Fielding voice begins to be heard in his first dramatic work.

As its title indicates, *Love in Several Masques* deals with the masks and disguises under which love conceals or manifests itself in the world, with the many ruses and subterfuges men and women resort to in their attempts to satisfy this most fundamental human need. Through a series of unmaskings, of peelings away of false perceptions and attitudes, the play aims to define true love and identify those who are worthy of it. With the possible exception of Merital, whose name suggests his already deserving nature, all the main characters must prove the sincerity and value of their pretensions to love. Merital is, in many ways, the norm they must emulate: he cannot marry Helena because of the interference of her uncle, the fatuous Sir Positive Trap; they cannot marry because of blocking agents within themselves. Wisemore has overcompensated for his past follies by becoming a world-weary misanthrope, a humorless plain dealer. Malvil has grown to resemble Wisemore without having to leave town, as a result of the failure of his romance with Vermilia. Lady Matchless does not wish to marry Wisemore because she still remembers her disastrous first marriage and is afraid of making the same mistake twice. Vermilia cannot accept Malvil because of his unreasonable jealousy and her own fears and misconceptions about love. Finally, Helena is capable of being deceived about Merital's intentions by her aunt's stratagems, but her deception, wholly due to external appearances and contrary to the true dictates of her heart, does not last long. She is a worthy mate for Merital.

Love in Several Masques, then, examines the pursuit and attainment of true love in the context of marriage. All three couples will be married at the end, but only one is psychologically ready from the beginning. The play traces the process by which these marriages will eventually come about by focusing most specifically on one of them—that between Lady Matchless and Wisemore—and using the other two as foils to it. In addition, Fielding is concerned not so much with his ladies as with his gentlemen. The gentlemen must prove their merit to the ladies; the ladies' merit, by their gallants' own admission, grudging as this admission may be in Malvil's case, is beyond dispute from the start. The opening scene establishes that Helena, Lady Matchless, and Vermilia are the best womankind has to offer; their suitors must present solid evidence— to the ladies, to the audience, to themselves—that they deserve to be wedded to these paragons. Fielding wants to define the ideal suitor and, in doing so, the ideal man. For this reason, he devotes the whole first act to the gentlemen. We see them before we see the ladies and thus become interested in their side of the story from the very beginning. Our initial acquaintance with the men is through their own words and actions; with the women, through the words and perceptions of the men. This is not a conceptual or structural flaw, the youthful Fielding's inability to bring description and representation into closer contact, but a dramatic strategy dictated by the thematic exigencies of the play.[19]

Although the best way to appreciate Fielding's achievement in *Love in Several Masques* might be to follow its plot as it unfolds, such a detailed analysis would take too long to rehearse. Moreover, the intricacies and complications of Fielding's first play, while testifying to his meticulous care in constructing his work, do not merit attention in themselves. For example, Fielding uses the number three as his main organizing principle. The play has three ladies, three men of sense, three fops, and three other characters. The three heroes meet their ladies three times; three times the women are compared to "garrisons"; three letters complicate and unravel the plot; and three dramatic unmaskings reveal the true identity of a disguised character. These "trinal triplicities"—to borrow Spenser's felicitous phrase—together with the use of verbal echoes and settings to implement specific thematic purposes, testify to the painstaking attention to detail and architectonics we tend to associate with the consummate craftsman of *Tom Jones*, not with the novice of the theater. Hume's judgment that "Fielding offers three minimally intertwined love plots," that "the design is clumsy," is unjust.[20] Still, a plot summary of *Love in Several Masques* would differ little from plot summaries of dozens of Restoration and eighteenth-century plays. Instead, we shall focus at this point on those concerns that would remain prominent throughout Fielding's dramatic career and return to the work in more detail during our discussion of *The Temple Beau*.

The close scrutiny of words and actions, the ability to read the world properly and thus arrive at correct judgments, the stripping away of masks to reveal the reality behind them—these are Fielding's concerns in *Love in Several Masques*. This model of observation and judgment—which recalls Locke's method of observation and reflection—is, of course, the theatrical model. The audience in the theater observes the action unfolding on stage and attempts to interpret it correctly, often with the help of the playwright, who reveals to his patrons crucial bits of information that he withholds from his characters. This theatrical model will later appear in the novels. For example, the reader of *Tom Jones*, apprised of Blifil's villainy from the beginning, might begin to suspect Allworthy's sagacity; but, as the narrator points out, Allworthy is not privy to this knowledge and can judge only from what he sees and hears. This is why the narrator, "by Way of Chorus," advises his "young Readers"—in a chapter aptly titled "In which the Author himself makes his Appearance on Stage" (3.7)—to make sure that their outward performances are consonant with their intentions. From the beginning of his dramatic career, Fielding emphasizes the theatricality of human action, whether on stage or in the world.[21] His characters act out roles and scenes that other characters attempt to interpret.

In the opening scene of *Love in Several Masques*, this dramatic procedure is explicitly enacted when Merital offers Malvil his de-

18

scription and interpretation of Lady Matchless's actions in the play-house on the previous night. Lady Matchless, it appears, is the play the audience have come to watch. She is the focus of attention, the cynosure of all eyes and ears. But, as Merital observes, she seems unaware that she is on stage—"seems" because Merital's phrasing suggests that Lady Matchless might be aware of her "performance": "Nor could all this [attention] elevate her to the least pride or haughtiness, but she *carried it with an air* not conscious of the envy and adoration she contracted. That becoming modesty in her eyes! that lovely, easy sweetness in her smile! that gracefulness in her mien! that nobleness, without affectation, in her looks!" (1.1 [16]; emphasis mine). Lady Matchless is a consummate actress, using art to conceal art. Later in the play she reveals her awareness of the close connection between world and stage: "There is more danger in woods and purling streams than in an assembly or a play-house. When a beauteous grove is your theatre, a murmuring cascade your music, nature's flowery landscapes your scene, heaven only the spectator, and a pretty fellow the actor—the Lord knows what the play will be" (2.1 [31]). As she shrewdly suggests, assemblies and playhouses are less dangerous because of their explicit theatricality. By the end it will turn out that her performance and her inner worth coincide; she is the genuine article and Merital has been a good understander (in Jonson's sense of the word) of her character.

Merital is indeed the most able interpreter in the play, though his own attempt to stage-manage a scene (3.13), because of his failure to control the response of his audience (Helena), meets with disastrous results. As we shall see, the importance of controlling the responses of an audience to a scene or play will be one of Fielding's guiding concerns in his subsequent drama, in particular his Scriblerian plays. Like Merital, Wisemore also views the world as a stage. He has "been a spectator of all [the] scenes" of London: "I have seen hypocrisy pass for religion, madness for sense, noise and scurrility for wit, and riches for the whole train of virtues. Then I have seen folly beloved for its youth and beauty, and reverenced for its age. I have discovered knavery in more forms than ever Proteus had, and traced him through them all" (1.2 [20]). While accurate in its own terms, Wisemore's assessment of the scenes of the capital is incomplete. He has both understood and misunderstood what he has seen. Wisemore sees folly and hypocrisy everywhere because that is what he wishes to see: his preconceptions cloud his judgment. All the forms, all the actions, all the scenes of London cannot be reduced to the single quality of knavery. The world of London might be presided over by Proteus, but he is not the only deity in town. Wisemore fails to understand that not all men and women—even in London's beau monde—are hypocrites, that some of them are acting out virtuous performances that mirror their inner goodness.

Wisemore's misunderstanding of London life can be traced to his reading habits. After living as an actor in the scenes of the city, Wisemore has retired to the country to study philosophy. He now finds that books are "a society preferable to that of this age." As he asks Merital, "Who would converse with fools and fops, whilst they might enjoy a Cicero or an Epictetus, a Plato, or an Aristotle?" (1.2 [19]). To ascertain that this is his "old friend metamorphosed, and no apparition," Merital sets out to "survey [him] a little" (ibid.). Merital's survey of Wisemore leads him to advise his friend not to "affect singularity this way." Merital has read his friend's character and arrived at the judgment that while Wisemore might be sincere in his new role, he should know that "in town we look on none to be so great a fool as a philosopher, and there is no fool so out of fashion" (p. 21). Fool or not, Wisemore is behaving foolishly by choosing to play the part of philosopher on the town stage. But Merital's gentle chiding of his friend's singularity goes beyond this hint on acting. Merital has discovered that his former companion might be affecting his singularity. Merital's reading of Wisemore's performance is accurate: as the plot unfolds, it is revealed that Wisemore's philosophical mask conceals a distressed lover, that he is not, as he claims, a "spectator" of the Protean scenes of the city but a votary of the god of metamorphosis, a participant and actor in the play from which he wishes to abstract himself.

The act of reading, then, provides Fielding with another model for the interpretation of human action; in subsequent works, this would become one of his favorite ways of defining the true nature of a character, by the books and authors he or she reads, or fails to read. In *The Temple Beau*, for example, Wilding is a law student who reads no law books; Shamela's miscellaneous library underscores the poverty of the furniture of her mind; and in *Amelia* (1751) Booth's vicissitudes and eventual "conversion" owe a large debt to his (and his creator's) reading.[22] Men and women read books, but, more important, they read each other. Throughout his dramatic career Fielding explores the complexities of this apparently simple analogy between the act of reading books and the observation of human action. Reading, properly done, combines seeing with understanding. In life as well as in the theater we often witness actions that we do not understand, either because those performing the actions wish to deceive us or because we do not make an effort to understand what we see. In either case—and there are many other possibilities—misunderstanding occurs because the observer stops at the surface, does not look behind or beyond the outward show, skims rather than peruses.

Fielding's aim in most of his plays, as we shall see, is to teach his audience to read dramatic action as though it were a difficult book, to scrutinize a performance on stage with the same care and effort demanded by the perusal of a puzzling text. Correct judgments can be reached only by examining and reexamining the evidence, by reflecting on what is seen or heard. Several years later, in *An Essay on the Knowledge of the Characters of Men*, Fielding would return to this important subject and set down rules for "discoveries." The passage in question, from which I quote at length, reads almost like a gloss on *Love in Several Masques*:

> Thus while the crafty and designing Part of Mankind, consulting only their own separate Advantage, endeavour to maintain one constant Imposition on others, the whole World becomes a vast Masquerade, where the greatest Part appear disguised under false Vizors and Habits; a very few only shewing their own Faces, who become, by so doing, the Astonishment and Ridicule of all the rest.
>
> But however cunning the Disguise be which a Masquerader wears: however foreign to his Age, Degree, or Circumstance, yet if closely attended to, he very rarely escapes the Discovery of an accurate Observer; for Nature, which unwillingly submits to the Imposture, is ever endeavouring to peep forth and shew herself; nor can the Cardinal, the Friar, or the Judge, long conceal the Sot, the Gamester, or the Rake.

> In the same Manner will those Disguises which are worn on the greater Stage, generally vanish, or prove ineffectual to impose the assumed for the real Character upon us, if we employ sufficient Diligence and Attention to the Scrutiny.[23]

The first reader we hear about in *Love in Several Masques* is Helena who, as Merital observes, "has improved by an intimate conversation with plays, poems, romances, and such gay studies, by which she has acquired a perfect knowledge of the polite world without ever seeing it, and turned the confinement of her person into the enlargement of her mind" (1.1 [17]). Merital's words look forward to the appearance of the second character in the play who has had "conversation" with the printed word. Unlike Helena, Wisemore has turned the confinement of his person into that of his mind. As noted, he is a reader of books but not of men. Happily he has chosen the right books to help him become a good man, though he has momentarily misunderstood them by taking to heart their renunciatory doctrines and believing that a virtuous life is incompatible with life in society.

At the other end of the spectrum lies Lord Formal, who reveals his intellectual and moral vacuity (to be truly moral a man must be fully aware) by advancing that "reading . . . is the worst thing in the world for the eyes" and professing, in a wonderful pun, that he reads only titles (1.5 [27]). He is such an example of consummate good breeding that Vermilia suspects that he has written a "book" on politeness (3.6 [49]). Sir Apish Simple, a lesser fop but a greater fool, prides himself on his modest knowledge of sartorial matters, telling Merital that he has "studied dress long enough to know a little" (4.10 [74]). Finally, Merital does not boast about his book knowledge, but he has nonetheless learned to read the world correctly, especially woman, "that noble volume of our greatest happiness." As he explains to Wisemore, "Women are like books. Malice and envy will easily lead you to the detection of their faults; but their beauties good judgment only can discover and good nature relish" (1.6 [29]). For this reason he advises Wisemore "to give over your attack, or change your method. For, be assured, widows are a study you will never be any proficient in, till you are initiated into that modern science which the French call *le bon assurance*" (4.9 [73]).

22

Wisemore must temper his philosophy with social grace; he must learn to read and act anew. Merit, an oft-repeated word in *Love in Several Masques* and Fielding's other plays signifying the quality that renders a man worthy of his mistress, consists in the perfect equipoise between good nature and good breeding, between inner excellence and outward performance. A man must possess very good judgment, must be a most acute reader and skilled performer, to achieve that equilibrium. By the end of the play Wisemore has learned the valuable lesson that men's complaints against women "flow generally (if not always) more from our want of merit than your want of justice" and offers "a solemn recantation" of all his "slanders" against the sex (5.14 [99]). With this compliment to the good judgment of the ladies, Wisemore shows that he has become a wise reader, not simply the reader of wise books, and that he is now ready to act his part as husband to Lady Matchless, the woman whose performance at the playhouse had raised Merital's admiration the night before he found himself describing and interpreting the scene to his friend Malvil, in the opening act of a new play being acted on the venerable stage of the Theatre Royal, Drury Lane, before an audience of reader-interpreters.

Fielding's second play to be acted, *The Temple Beau*, opened at Goodman's Fields on 26 January 1730 after being rejected by the managers at Drury Lane and perhaps at Lincoln's Inn Fields; it ran for nine nights.[24] The change in locale is significant because with few exceptions Fielding's plays were not acted in the patent houses but in the smaller fringe establishments, most notably the Little Theatre in the Haymarket. Free from the restrictions and expectations of the legitimate theater of the licensed playhouses, Fielding could experiment as he wished. These experiments would begin with his next play, *The Author's Farce*. *The Temple Beau*, however, appeared in a house which, though built by Thomas Odell in 1729 away from the fashionable theater district, among the merchants in Whitechapel, nonetheless specialized in traditional dramatic forms. As A. H. Scouten has written of this period, "For the first time since Charles II had issued patents at the beginning of the Restoration three regular companies were playing legitimate drama in

London."[25] Fielding's play was accepted because it was traditional legitimate drama.

The central character of *The Temple Beau* is Wilding, a young man who has forsaken his legal studies to pursue the pleasures of the town. His role as protagonist of the play signals an important shift from *Love in Several Masques*. Fielding is still concerned with defining the good man as he who merits to marry the judicious (and rich) woman at the end; but, since Veromil is already that good man, and Valentine exists only to enhance Veromil's excellence by his impulsive behavior, that concern is secondary. Instead, Fielding focuses on the actions of his reprehensible characters, Lady Gravely, Lady Pedant, and, of course, Wilding. Wilding is wicked and hypocritical, but in spite of his arrant rascality we follow his machinations with interest, if not with sympathy. We wish him success in gulling his father and Lady Gravely. He loses our support only when he expresses his desire to marry Bellaria exclusively for her wealth, especially since we know that she and Veromil are made for each other. Fielding's main interest in *The Temple Beau*, then, is not so much with love as with hypocrisy. However, since his hypocritical characters are so transparent in their dissembling, since their false posturings are so obvious, Fielding treats them with Horatian mildness. Like the fops in *Love in Several Masques*, they are not embodiments of evil but the innocuous objects of comic laughter. As James Ralph writes in the prologue to the play, "The comic muse, in smiles severely gay, / Shall scoff at vice, and laugh its crimes away."[26]

Because of its simpler plot *The Temple Beau* is easier to follow than *Love in Several Masques*. The structural complexities of Fielding's first play can be appreciated only by scrutinizing virtually every scene, every speech, every word. Strands of its several subplots weave in and out through thirteen scene changes. *The Temple Beau*, on the other hand, develops almost in a straight line, with its five scene changes corresponding to natural breaks in the action. *The Temple Beau*, in other words, usually carries a particular set of events to its conclusion before moving on to another; *Love in Several Masques* freezes one subplot at a certain point, then turns to another and advances it until it catches up with the first one, then continues with the initial subplot or turns to yet another one, and so on. *Love in Several Masques* builds through the intertwining of discrete frames, *The Temple Beau* by the accretion of larger sequences. The former play, though effective on the stage, delights more those who enjoy discovering structural intricacies in the privacy of their closets; the latter, by recognizing that there is a limit to how many fragments of a story an audience in the theater can be reasonably expected to hold in suspension, makes for better acting drama.

If Fielding worked with triads in *Love in Several Masques*, in *The Temple Beau* he uses doublets. The absence of one variable in the dramatic equation accounts, to a large extent, for the relative simplicity of the later play. It also allows Fielding to maintain a tighter grip on his central theme by drawing sharper pictures, offering starker contrasts. Of all the characters only Pincet, Wilding's servant, stands without a mate. Sir Avarice Pedant and Sir Harry Wilding are the two old guardians whose view of marriage is purely economical; Lady Lucy Pedant and Lady Gravely represent two different yet complementary sides of the same hypocritical coin; and Wilding and Young Pedant recall each other in their contrasting attitudes toward, and use of, book learning. There are no longer three couples whose fortunes we must follow, but two, Bellaria-Veromil and Clarissa-Valentine. While *Love in Several Masques* ramifies, *The Temple Beau* pares down.

But the process of attenuation does not stop here. Valentine, because of his uncontrollable passion for Bellaria, soon loses our sympathy. Clarissa is so insubstantial as almost to escape our attention. Their love story affects us little; they exist only as foils to Bellaria and Veromil. This couple, for their part, do not capture our imagination with the same force as Merital and Helena: their eventual marriage is even more of a foregone conclusion. The spotlight must, of necessity, fall on Wilding. A closer comparison with *Love in Several Masques* will clarify this point.

In *Love in Several Masques* we are interested in all three couples, but our main concern is reserved for Wisemore and Lady Matchless. In *The Temple Beau* that central marriage never happens. We are left with a vacuum at the center, a vacuum that can be filled only by Wilding. He, in other words, corresponds to Wisemore in the earlier play, as Valentine does to Malvil, Veromil to Merital, Bellaria to Helena, and Clarissa to Vermilia. Vermilia is more memorable than Clarissa, and Malvil more admirable than Valentine, but the analogies are still valid, especially when one remembers that Valentine and Malvil, as Fielding once again glances in the direction of *The Conscious Lovers*, share a fondness for dueling.

That Fielding intends us to think of Wisemore and Wilding as related characters emerges from the striking similarities between their introductions in their respective plays. In *Love in Several Masques*, as Fielding recalls the opening scene of Farquhar's *The Constant Couple*, Merital and Malvil are discussing their amorous fortunes when Merital describes the approaching Wisemore (1.1); in *The Temple Beau* Veromil and Valentine are engaged in a similar conversation when Veromil sees Wilding (1.6). Wisemore is described as having been "metamorphosed" (p. 19) from a man about town into a man of letters. Wilding has undergone the opposite transformation: he has "altered" (p. 115) into a fop since his presumably studious days at the university. Both men have changed their habits, in dress as well as in reading; both men, as their newly donned costumes reveal, are playing different roles on the town stage. The differences between Wisemore and Wilding, then, contribute considerably to the changes in method and emphasis between the two plays.

These changes are evident from the start. *The Temple Beau* opens with a quarrel between Lady Lucy Pedant, Sir Avarice's young wife, and her sister-in-law, the twice-widowed Lady Gravely, whose name points not only to her affected gravity but also to her lethal effect on her husbands. The scene—which may have been modeled on the confrontation between Arsinoé and Célimène in Molière's *Misanthrope* (3.5)—does not provide any background information, as does the first section of *Love in Several Masques*, but rather establishes a context of hypocrisy for the ensuing drama. Each woman, unaware of her own shortcomings or, what is more likely, pretending not to have any, confronts the other with the unflattering portrait the town paints of her character. Lady Gravely assures her sister that "the world gives you the honour of being the most finished coquette in town" (1.1 [107]), while Lady Pedant expresses the common view that Lady Gravely's "actions are as much disguised by [her] words, as [her] skin by paint"

26

(p. 105). Lady Pedant is a flirt, and Lady Gravely an aging, hypocritical prude. Both women will validate the accuracy of these portraits in their intrigues with Wilding.

The hypocrisy of the women in Sir Avarice's household is further underscored in the scene in which Bellaria is introduced. When Bellaria discloses that she loves a man (she does not mention his name) because of his "merit," Lady Gravely upbraids her for her "immodesty" and Lady Pedant ridicules her for her "stupidity" (2.7 [124]). Bellaria recognizes that she cannot please both her aunts because she will never "come up" to the "gravity" of one or to the "gaeity" of the other (p. 126). Lady Pedant wants her to go to plays and assemblies to complete her "education," while Lady Gravely suggests that she attend church. Bellaria chooses a via media: "I dare venture to both—I shall never reach that sublime way of thinking, which imputes dulness to that, or levity to this" (ibid.). Bellaria rejects the "sublime way of thinking" because of its dangers, its artificiality, its hypocrisy. Bellaria's honesty is nowhere more evident than in her dealings with Veromil. As she tells Clarissa, she considers hiding one's passion for a worthy man a "ridiculous cruelty," "as monstrous a folly as 'tis a barbarity" (5.4 [168]). She believes that "over-coquetry is but a gilt cover over a volume of nonsense, which will be despised by all wise men" (ibid.).[27] Wise men, in this context, are those acute readers who, like Veromil, reject all but the most edifying books and love only the most deserving of women, women whose actions are not hypocritical performances but revelations of their inner goodness.

Unlike their virtuous niece, Lady Pedant and Lady Gravely relish the dissimulations that accompany the satisfaction of a guilty passion. Bellaria's "gilt," in this sense, may convey more than she intends. Lady Pedant is conducting an affair with Wilding with characteristic insouciance. She does not fully admit to herself that her affair is culpable because, on the one hand, it is out in the open, the fashionable thing to do for a young woman saddled with an old fool, and, on the other, it has apparently not been physically consummated. She is hypocritical not so much to others as to herself: she hides behind her adherence to the rules of the beau monde— or at least the conventions of Restoration comedy—and the du-

27

bious comfort of a sexual technicality. For her part, Lady Gravely conceals her lust, like Molière's Tartuffe, under the cloak of religion and morality.

If Lady Lucy, Lady Gravely, and Wilding are conscious hypocrites, actors aware of their false performances, Young Pedant is a pretender who fails to recognize that he is pretending. At his father's instigation he will court Bellaria and thus become a reluctant rival both to Veromil and to Wilding. He claims to have read much, but he has absorbed little. He burdens his conversation with constant allusions to the classics, but his allusions are so commonplace that they betray the superficiality of his acquaintance with their sources. He is an example of arrested development, the professional student who, like Trofimov in Chekhov's *Cherry Orchard*, refuses to abandon the false security of the academy. Most of his contemporaries at the university have exchanged their books for other pursuits. Valentine, for example, observes that, as a student, he had been deprived of the "pleasantest part of knowledge . . . woman; a sort of books prohibited at the university" (1.5 [114]). Valentine, Veromil, and Wilding have changed their reading habits, while Young Pedant clings desperately to his. Only bad readers, Fielding seems to suggest, fail to note when books have outlived their usefulness; only bad readers refuse to grow up and experience love and the world.

misreading

There are, of course, degrees of misreading and categories of misreaders. Valentine has renounced all books and now devotes his time to foppish fashions and to the pursuit of women, especially the pursuit of the one woman who does not love him. Wilding reads plays and Rochester's poems, as befits a young rake, not the law books his father expects him to read. Veromil has not given up reading altogether but studies only those subjects that contribute to the making of a good man, as his homilies to Valentine on friendship, honor, the duties of a Christian, and love amply demonstrate (4.10). Indeed, a measure of the epistemological gap between Veromil and Young Pedant may be seen in their understanding of the word *providence*, a word that appears only twice in the play. Veromil views providence as the benevolent ordering of the world that will eventually bring about his marriage to Bellaria (2.11 [129]). Young Pedant hopes that if he has to marry Bellaria to avoid being disinherited, he "(providentially) . . . may get rid of [his] wife" (1.4 [114]). For him, providence is the agent that destroys those who get in our way. His conception of the term is so narrow and distorted that it is small enough to fit, as an adverb, in parentheses. The supreme triumph of his erudition occurs at the center of the play, when Bellaria leaves him to his "meditations," as he attempts to woo her by demonstrating "obedience to a parent" with an endless catalogue of learned citations (3.6 [143–44]). He does not know that he is addressing the winds until Valentine wakes him from his classical trance and stops his ranting (3.8). His soliloquy (3.7) epitomizes the impotence and solitariness of a man who pursues knowledge without wisdom.

In *The Temple Beau*, then, Fielding exposes the impotence of villainy, the shallow rewards of hypocrisy, the true ridiculous underlying the posturings of vanity and affectation. He thus focuses on the plots and counterplots of several characters who succeed only in fooling each other and themselves. Their machinations fail because these plotters, forgetting that they are characters in a play, mere puppets in a puppet show, have sought to usurp the providential office of the dramatist. As we shall see, Fielding would explore the subject of competing plots and playwrights in greater depths in subsequent plays like *Rape upon Rape*. What was a conventional and, through repetition, a hackneyed feature of regular comedy would become a major device in Fielding's dramatic practice, a device he would use to probe the complexities, indeed the very nature, of theatrical illusion.

As *The Temple Beau* concludes with Veromil's providential platitude that "heaven" means "to reward the virtuous and the great" (p. 187), Wilding remains unrepentant. Yet his failure to marry Bellaria and his inability to consummate his illicit passions with Lady Pedant and Lady Gravely underscore his essential harmlessness. His pledge to satisfy Lady Gravely with more "substantial reasons" (ibid.) acts as an ironic reminder that, while he may pretend to be a ladies' man, he has yet to succeed in going beyond clumsy and ill-fated foreplay, as when Sir Avarice Pedant foils his attempts to embrace Lady Lucy (3.1–2). In other words, Fielding has allowed Wilding to boast as much as he desires, but has never permitted him to show, on stage, any solid evidence to support his extravagant claims. He is no Horner, but a protean, inconsequential, bungling poseur. Like Young Pedant, he cannot manage to engage in any "substantial" conversation with the ladies. He can only triumph over his father. But, given Sir Harry's mental opacity and moral turpitude, this is a hollow victory at best.

It would not be until *The Modern Husband* (1732) that Fielding would deal more realistically with the question of evil and face it squarely as an undeniable trait of the human animal. For now, however, he was content with depicting the ethically objectionable man as a lusus naturae, as the scapegoat cast out at the providentially appointed happy ending. In short, he was still satisfied with presenting a traditional comic situation within a conventional framework, with appending happy endings, in Cibberian fashion, to his plays. *The Temple Beau* may differ from *Love in Several Masques* in method and in thematic emphasis, but both plays can still be recognized as typical variations on the five-act comedy of the Restoration and the early eighteenth century. Fielding may have been a more conscious craftsman than many of his predecessors and contemporaries, but he had not yet done anything to distinguish himself from them. He was still working in their shadows, with their tools, speaking with their inflections. All that would change with his next play: the apprentice would begin to find his own dramatic voice.

CHAPTER 2

The Apprentice Finds His Voice:
The Author's Farce (1730)

FIELDING'S FIRST IRREGULAR play, *The Author's Farce*, began its initial run of forty-one performances at the Little Theatre in the Haymarket on 30 March 1730.[1] While its spectacular success established Fielding's reputation in the London theatrical world, it must have also confirmed some of his worst fears about the declining taste of the public and the fate of new regular drama. His own experience vouched for that grim assessment. His first play had received only moderate acclaim and, as he must have realized, it could very easily have been rejected because the actor-managers at Drury Lane, struggling to survive against the entertainments mounted by John Rich at Lincoln's Inn Fields—most recently the fabulously popular *Beggar's Opera*—had begun not only to put on entertainments of their own but also to confine their productions of regular plays almost exclusively to revivals of old standards from Congreve, Etherege, Farquhar, Wycherley, and (with increasing frequency) Shakespeare.[2] New playwrights, no matter how talented and promising they might be, had little chance of getting a fair hearing for their work, let alone of seeing it acted. Samuel Madden's complaint, in the preface to *Themistocles, the Lover of his Country* (1729), is representative of the doleful rhetoric of disappointed new authors: "With all its Faults, I did not think this Piece deserv'd so severe Treatment, as to be peremptorily refused, after the most earnest and early Sollicitations, at the Old House for two Winters together. . . . Take Notice, that if Mr. *Dryden*, Mr. *Otway*, or Mr. *Southern* (whose first Plays were so vastly short of their following ones) had been so severely discouraged by the Managers of the Theatre, as Gentlemen are now, our Country had possibly wanted those great Ornaments of the Stage for ever" (p. v).

Given the evidence of his tragic piece, Madden was no ornament, but his words, had Fielding read them, would have rung true. Although the situation for new authors, in actual fact, had begun to improve by 1729, with the challenge to the licensed playhouses mounted by the Little Haymarket, there was nonetheless a limited market for new regular plays, especially at Drury Lane.[3] Simply stated, a new regular play, even if it succeeded, was not likely to reward the managers. Thus the author of *The Laureat*—admittedly a hostile witness—after offering "an Account of the Manner of introducing a new Play on the Stage during the Government of these three Theatrical Administrators," recalls that "*Booth* has, with great Frankness, often publickly declared at *Button*'s, that they did not design or desire to act any new Play, whether it was good or bad; and he gave the true and natural Reason for it, which was, that their House was always full, and therefore they must loose whenever the Profits of a third or sixth Night were on this Occasion deducted" (pp. 94–96). The initial rejection of *The Temple Beau* by Cibber and Wilks must have finally convinced Fielding that if he wanted to succeed in the theater, he had to strike out in a different direction. Gay had apparently capitulated by submitting a play to Rich which, whatever its satiric intentions, had struck a responsive chord in the man to whom, in Fielding's words, "we owe (if not the invention) at least the bringing into fashion, that sort of writing which [he has] pleased to distinguish by the name of Entertainment."[4] The result of this unlikely alliance had been the thundering applause of the town and the monetary comfort of manager and playwright. If Gay could do it, Fielding must have reasoned, so could he.

C. B. Woods has remarked that "it would be difficult to exaggerate the importance of *The Author's Farce* in Fielding's dramatic career; its position is somewhat analogous to that of *Shamela* and *Joseph Andrews* with respect to his development as a writer of prose fiction."[5] Wilbur Cross has stressed its significance by noting that when Fielding eschewed the traditional five-act comedy of the Restoration to please a Haymarket audience nurtured on coarse, highly

32

physical satiric productions as well as the even less heady fare of dancers, tumblers, and opera singers, "it was soon apparent . . . that [his] talent really lay in farce and burlesque rather than in regular drama."[6] These two observations are essentially sound but need to be qualified.

The Author's Farce looms large in Fielding's dramatic career and development principally from the vantage point of his later triumphs in irregular drama. When one looks back from *Pasquin* (1736) and *The Historical Register for the Year 1736* (1737), *The Author's Farce* certainly seems to anticipate and foreshadow. The only problem with this view is that it fails to take into account that despite this apparent breakthrough in his third acted play, Fielding continued to write five-act comedies. Was he so insensitive to his own talents that he persisted in attempting a type of drama for which he was poorly fitted? That may be, though an analysis of his regular plays shows that he was far from inept in that genre; scholars who think otherwise have not examined these plays very carefully. I wish to suggest instead that Fielding kept returning to regular forms because he believed that he would eventually achieve his potential as a dramatist in them, that he would demonstrate his merit as a playwright by taking the structures and plots he had inherited from his predecessors and making them new by imbuing them with his own artistic ether. He may have begun to see the impossibility of that dream, especially after the less than enthusiastic reception of *The Modern Husband*, which he always considered his best contribution to the genre, and abandoned it altogether by the time he came to write the final irregular plays. But this hypothesis seems to be undermined by his references in the preface to the *Miscellanies* (1743) to the viability of five-act comedies.[7] Of course, that prefatory matter was written six years after the official ending of his theatrical exertions, when the pendulum of dramatic affairs, aided by the Licensing Act's curtailment of daring experiment and Garrick's histrionic virtuosity in traditional forms, had swung once again toward regularity; by then Fielding might have changed his mind once more. Still, the point remains that when he wrote *The Author's Farce*, he could not have known that he was adumbrating later developments in his dramatic career.

In 1730, then, *The Author's Farce* signaled an important change from Fielding's previous practice and nothing more. In retrospect we might be tempted to attribute prophetic significance to that change. If we do so we shall be committing the teleological fallacy and distorting the facts. This factual distortion—so long as we recognize it as such and seek a truer apprehension of the issues involved—can nonetheless enhance our understanding of Fielding's dramatic career. We cannot deny, after all, that *The Author's Farce* exhibits many of the features of his later irregular drama, that it is, in many ways, the prototype of what was to come. It is in this particular sense that I intend my remarks about Fielding "finding his voice." To a large extent Fielding found his voice with every play he wrote, but the sound of that voice became louder and clearer when he turned from the traditional structures and procedures of his first two plays and created his own in the third. At the same time, we must not forget that there is another side to be explored, that the significance of *The Author's Farce* lies not only in what it led to but also in what it was leading from. From that perspective, the play's formal shift becomes not so much an example of proleptic dramaturgy but the product of artistic accommodation, Fielding's partial capitulation to the demands and taste of the public.

The full title of the play—*The Author's Farce and the Pleasures of the Town*—begins to suggest the nature of Fielding's concessions to popular diversions. We must grant, first of all, that Fielding is explicitly aiming to ridicule the contemporary infatuation with opera, pantomime, puppet shows, and other similar spectacles, that his intent is satiric from the start.[8] This is why he indicates that the work has been written by Scriblerus Secundus, a cognomen linking him to the satirical lucubrations of the Scriblerus Club of Arbuthnot, Gay, Pope, and Swift. In accordance with Scriblerian practice, Fielding incorporates into his play those very elements he wishes to attack; that is, he lures his audience into the theater by offering them precisely those amusements they are so fond of. He then pays his spectators the further compliment of making them believe, by allowing them to share his satiric stance, that they are not the objects of his derision, that they, unlike other contemporary audiences, can discriminate good art from bad. We are always willing to have our pleasures castigated, Fielding seems to have under-

34

stood, so long as the castigation is good natured and it is somehow agreed that we are not really so stupid and wicked as we appear: we rarely look in the satiric mirror and see our own faces. Fielding himself does not escape unscathed. He might protest his satiric intent as justification for parading puppets on his stage, but the ineluctable fact remains that he has stooped to this device to attract unsuspecting members of the public under false pretenses, that he has participated in the corruption of art he is purporting to chastise, that he has compromised his craft to make money. To understand what Fielding was up to, the dangers he was incurring, the accommodations he was making, we must examine the structure of his play and the motives of his protagonist, his namesake and brother dramatist Harry Luckless.

The Author's Farce consists of two parts. The first, comprising acts one and two, deals with the romantic and monetary vicissitudes of the impecunious Harry Luckless. The second, act three, presents Luckless's gambit to rescue himself from his financial misfortunes, the puppet show enacting the "pleasures of the town." The play seems to start off as a conventional love comedy—indeed, Fielding may have borrowed his opening scenes from act three of Farquhar's *Love and a Bottle*—except for the curious fact that its hero, like Valentine in Congreve's *Love for Love*, is a playwright. Mrs. Moneywood's opening line—"Never tell me, Mr. Luckless, of your play, and your play" (p. 7)—emphasizes Luckless's occupation and poverty from the beginning. His courtship of Harriot is subordinated to his theatrical endeavors, and these endeavors, in turn, are inextricably bound up with his efforts to achieve fame and financial independence. If merit in *Love in Several Masques* and *The Temple Beau* refers primarily to that quality which renders a man worthy of a virtuous woman, here it denotes literary excellence. Witmore and Marplay, whose views on the subject are otherwise antithetical, agree that merit has little weight in an age when "party and prejudice carry all before them" (1.5 [16]), when "interest sways as much in the theatre as at court" (2.2 [26]). Like the heroines of Fielding's two previous comedies, Harriot uses the word to signify what makes Luckless her deserving partner. She despises the "fool" who is born to wealth but admires "the man who, thrown naked upon the world like my dear Luckless, can make his way through it by his merit and virtuous industry" (2.10 [37]). Merit, for Harriot, is no longer a purely intellectual and spiritual characteristic, as it is for Helena and Bellaria, but a man's ability to earn a living through his work; virtue, for her, is not a substantive abstraction but an adjectival adjunct of solid industry.

The redefinition of merit is closely connected with the modification of another familiar theme. The importance of correct reading in Fielding's first two plays is now supplemented with the concern with writing, first with writing well, and then, after that fails, with writing to the moment, for a sizable profit. Judging by its only speech cited in *The Author's Farce* (2.1 [24]), Luckless's first play, from which, as he tells Mrs. Moneywood, he has "great expectations" (1.2 [10]), appears to be a traditional five-act love comedy.[9] Its language, in fact, recalls that of the romantic interludes between Luckless and Harriot. In act two, scene three, for instance, the playwright and his beloved speak in verse or burst into song, as Fielding begins to experiment with ballad opera whenever their sentiments become too lofty for prose. When Luckless, after enumerating several possible calamities, asks Harriot how much more she will endure for "constant love," she replies,

> Oh, more than this, my Luckless, would I do.
> All places are a heaven when with you.
> Let me repose but on that faithful breast.
> Give me thy love, the world may take the rest.
> (1.3 [12])

The excerpt from Luckless's play rings changes on the same topos:

> Then hence my sorrows, hence my every fear,
> No matter where, so we are blessed together.
> With thee, the barren rocks, where not one step
> Of human race lies printed in the snow,
> Look lovely as the smiling infant spring.
> (2.1 [24])

As with Stephen Dedalus's villanelle in Joyce's *Portrait*, we cannot be entirely sure whether the author intends to poke fun at the aesthetic pretensions of his protagonist. Luckless's speech resembles those in Fielding's conventional comedies, though few of them are in verse, as well as the more tender exchanges in *The Author's Farce*. Moreover, Marplay's suggested emendations of it seem to argue for its soundness. Marplay, as he candidly confides to Sparkish, cannot recognize a piece of good writing: "It may be a very good one for aught I know" (2.2 [26]). An author cannot have a better indicator of his true worth than Marplay's rejection. The man's very name proclaims his critical obtuseness. Finally, Witmore, who is not a fool, seems to be convinced of his friend's artistic merit (p. 16).

The satire cuts both ways, however. While it may be true that Marplay is a bad critic, his method does not preclude his acceptance of a good play. He only cares about the author's "interest"; all other considerations are, at best, secondary. His corrections of Luckless's speech no doubt reflect his literary loutishness, but they also underscore how close to the "profund of Scriblerus"—to use Pope's phrase from the recent *Peri Bathous* (1728)—the young man's lines really lie. A push, ever so slight, will send Luckless's effusions tumbling down into the abyss of bathos. Marplay's revisions—"horror" for "sorrows," "so somewhere we're together" for "so we are blessed together"—stress the triteness of the original expressions. One formula can easily replace another. Luckless's fragment treads a well-worn path through dramatic history; Marplay's final *reductio ad absurdum* of its central image exposes the poverty of thought, the lack of invention, concealed under Luckless's rhetorical felicity. Fielding wanted regular drama to survive but realized that that survival could be ensured only by acknowledging and eliminating its many shortcomings, especially its susceptibility to endless and unimaginative repetitions of clichés and commonplaces.

Luckless's first play thus acts both as example and as caveat to contemporary advocates of traditional forms. It also serves as Fielding's dispassionate evaluation of certain potentially disastrous tendencies in his own writing, though he seldom devoted his energies to a romantic situation without tempering it with less sentimental comic emphases. In this respect *Love in Several Masques* is an atypical Fielding play, while *The Temple Beau* and *The Author's Farce* exemplify his usual practice of subsuming the love story under other thematic concerns. Even though their avowed purposes and motives are wrongheaded, then, Marplay and Sparkish, and their counterparts in the real world, Cibber and Wilks, are partly justified in snubbing plays that continue to parrot the conventions. Fielding venerated the old drama, but he was far from tolerant of those who persisted in playing hackneyed variations on it. The flaccid and predictable "wit traps" of Cibber had replaced the sinewy true wit of Wycherley and Congreve. Fielding was honest enough to recognize his own lapses into Cibberian "Pleasantry," as he would call it in the preface to *Plutus*, and he tried to rectify his method. The callous dissection and repudiation of Luckless's play may allude to the rejection of *The Temple Beau*, may indeed be an emblematic representation of the travails of regular drama when confronted by interest-ridden, functionally illiterate theatrical managers, but it is also a clarion call for change. And change was something both Fielding and Luckless were willing to attempt.

The most obvious change between Fielding's first two plays and *The Author's Farce* is that the latter, as its title indicates, is a farce, while the former two are comedies. In his preface to *The What D'ye Call It* (1715), a "tragi-comi-pastoral farce" combining a rehearsal with a play within a play and incongruously juxtaposing a serious plot with its ludicrous language and presentation, Gay argues that the "nature of Farce" is "that it is made up of absurdities and incongruities" and that, unlike comedy, it introduces episodes "without any coherence with the rest of the piece."[10] Farce is further distinguished by its low language and low characters and its reliance on slapstick rather than verbal wit to evoke mirth. In Thomas Wilkes's view, its popularity also offers evidence of a "vitiated appetite":

> Farce is founded on chimera and improbability; the events are unnatural, the humour forced, and it is, in the opinion of Dryden, a compound of extravagancies, fit only to entertain such people as are judges of neither men nor manners: it appeals entirely to the fancy; delights with oddity, and unexpected turns: it has in one thing indeed the same effect as Comedy, viz. it produces laughter; but it is not laughter founded upon reason, excited by the check given to folly, the reproof to ignorance, or the lash to corruption. Perhaps, if we enquire into the natural cause of the pleasure we feel from Farce, we shall find it to be the same that leads women to feed on chalk, and make dirt-pies; a vitiated

appetite: but this is so common, that he, who writes down to it, stands a better chance of pleasing, than he whose refined genius excels in painting nature, and exhibiting probability. It is, however, a species of the Drama very difficult to be carried into execution; great nicety being requisite to link improbabilities in such a manner, that they shall not disgust.[11]

Farce, in short, is inherently not the most intellectual or decorous of dramatic forms, though Fielding, following Gay's lead, would radically alter its aims and emphases.

During the Restoration and eighteenth century, farce was looked down upon because it apparently had no classical precedent and was not, therefore, a legitimate genre. Several writers, most notably Nahum Tate, justified their practice by reference to farcical elements in the comedies of Aristophanes and Plautus.[12] Others eloquently denounced farces, as Dryden does in his preface to *An Evening's Love: or, The Mock Astrologer* (1671), while succumbing to popular demand and writing them. The form, while still regarded as low, childish, and, as Wilkes's sexist analogy suggests, effeminate, had achieved a certain degree of legitimacy by Fielding's time, proving that in the theater at least the audience adjudicates as to how it wishes to be entertained, and playwrights, if they have any regard for their purses, invariably oblige. In the prologue to *The Lottery. A Farce* (1732), Fielding also advances a less mercenary reason for resorting to farce. Unlike comedy, which "delights to punish fools," "farce challenges the vulgar as her prize." While "some follies scarce perceptible appear/In that just glass which shows you as you are,"

> Farce still claims a magnifying right
> To raise the object larger to the sight,
> And show her insect fools in stronger light.[13]

This is perhaps why, in *The Author's Farce*, "the pleasures of the town" are represented in a magnified, life-size puppet show performed by actors and actresses who, through their puppetlike gestures, magnify the folly of all those presumably rational human beings who allow themselves to be mindlessly manipulated by the purveyors of intellectually vacuous entertainments.

Fielding had another important model in the tradition: Mo-

39

lière. Molière had served his apprenticeship as an actor principally in adaptations of commedia dell'arte, and most of his plays, usually written to be performed by his own company, with Molière himself in one of the leading roles, relied on the techniques and materials of the Italian comic theater.[14] Fielding would imitate Molière's manner more closely later in his career, in *The Mock Doctor* (1732), *The Miser* (1733), and *The Intriguing Chambermaid* (1734), but that direct imitation would constitute only a more overt acknowledgment of a debt that started early and continued to inform his artistic life. In *Tom Jones*, for example, Molière is cited as part of a catalogue of eminent authors inspired by "Genius"; Fielding invokes that deity to grant him, as she once did to Aristophanes, Lucian, Cervantes, Rabelais, Molière, Shakespeare, Swift, and Marivaux, the boon to "fill my Pages with Humour; till Mankind learn the Good-Nature to laugh only at the Follies of others, and the Humility to grieve at their own."[15] In Molière and his other comic precursors, Fielding found warrant for his own brand of benevolent comedy. In Molière in particular, he also discovered a source for using farce for purposes other than the mere stimulation of senseless guffaws and knee-slappings. He saw that farce could be employed to teach as well as to entertain. In *The Author's Farce*, then, Fielding would satisfy the public's desire for low spectacles, for mindless horseplay, without renouncing his didactic intent, without abdicating his responsibility as a serious artist. He would also attain fame and make a little money on the side.

The Janus-like nature of *The Author's Farce*, with its mixture of popular entertainments and traditional dramatic forms, its compromise between artistic and financial considerations, may be further explored in terms of Bookweight's distinction between *acting* and *reading* plays. As he explains to Witmore and Luckless, "Why, sir, your acting play is entirely supported by the merit of the actor, without any regard to the author at all. In this case, it signifies very little whether there be any sense in it or no. Now your reading play is of a different stamp and must have wit and meaning in it. These latter I call your substantive, as being able to support themselves. The former are your adjective, as what require the buffoonery and gestures of an actor to be joined to them to show their signification" (1.6 [18]).[16] One of the problems with Luckless's first

40

dramatic effort is that it is a reading play. It is concerned primarily with achieving a certain mellifluousness, a certain preciosity of style, and virtually neglects its theatrical possibilities. To some extent this had been the case with *Love in Several Masques*, whose complex structure betrays a relative degree of naiveté about stagecraft. What reads well in the study, what delights us with formal and verbal intricacies, does not necessarily translate into a successful evening in the playhouse. *Love in Several Masques* owed its moderate run to the performing talents of the Drury Lane company as much as it did to Fielding's writing.

At the other end of the spectrum lie the acting plays. In a most important respect, all drama belongs to this category because plays, by definition, are meant to be acted: the script has little dramatic value until fleshed out by the actors on the stage. To quote Molière's dictum: "Much depends on the acting." Fielding himself had become aware of this theatrical tenet, if he had not done so before, by the time he composed *The Wedding Day* (ca. 1730; acted in 1742). As he reveals in the preface to the *Miscellanies*, he had "intended" the "Parts of Millamour and Charlotte" in that play "for Mr. *Wilks* and Mrs. *Oldfield*."[17] Later he would write *The Intriguing Chambermaid* specifically to suit the histrionic genius of Kitty Clive. In analyzing plays, we often forget this crucial dimension. "Merital, Malvil, a buss, dear boys. Ha! hum! what figure is that?" (*Love in Several Masques*, 1.3 [22]) is a rather unremarkable line, until we remember that it was uttered by Colley Cibber. His consummate skill and fame as a stage fop, which often spilled over into his more quotidian transactions, coupled with his being a bit too old to impersonate a young beau, must have contributed to the ludicrousness of his portrayal and made an otherwise common piece of dialogue burst into uproarious life. Imagine the aging Cibber strutting the boards in full foppish regalia, as he effeminately asks for a buss in a high-pitched voice and gawks in disbelief at the rustic apparition before him. Moments like this not only define an acting play but capture the very essence of what the theater is about.

Acting plays, however, as Bookweight uses the term, also refer to those totally mindless popular entertainments that rely solely on the abilities of their performers to accomplish their purpose. *Hurlothrumbo: or, the Super-natural* (1729), for instance, makes little sense to a modern reader sitting in the North Library of the British Museum, who may rightly wonder what the original audiences at the Haymarket saw in this hopeless farrago. What they saw, and applauded, for thirty-two nights was the improbable acting of its "Ingenious Author," Samuel Johnson of Cheshire (1691–1773) who, as remarked in a footnote to James Miller's *Harlequin-Horace: or, the Art of Modern Poetry* (1731), "perform'd the Principal Part [Lord Flame], and danc'd, sung, and play'd on the Fiddle all at once."[18] This is the kind of play Witmore ironically advises Luckless to write if he wishes to please a contemporary audience (p. 16). It was also the type of amusement to which Haymarket patrons were accustomed. Fielding would satisfy their taste for the absurd and modify their expectations and perceptions by giving them an acting play with substance. Bookweight's distinction thus helps to locate *The Author's Farce* between two extreme coordinates on the contemporary theatrical map. Fielding came to recognize that a reading play, which he seems to identify with the conventional drama of the Restoration, could not answer the needs of a public clamoring for acting plays. Acting plays, for their part, because of their intellectual vacuity, were anathema to a serious artist. Fielding had to find a way to mediate between these two extremes. *The Author's Farce* succeeded because it was an acting play, most prominently in its third act. That we are still examining it today, acknowledging its merit and didactic intent, testifies to its status as a reading play.

One of the techniques Fielding uses to prevent *The Author's Farce* from degenerating into a mindless acting play is double satire. If we separate the work into two parts, as its title suggests, we end up with a frame consisting of the life of Harry Luckless and, within that frame, we find the puppet show depicting the pleasures of the town. Note, however, that the life of Harry Luckless acts as a frame only because it encloses the seemingly more fictive, more artificial puppet show. Were the play to deal exclusively with Luckless's difficulties, the whole piece would be fiction. But when Luckless presents his own play in the final section, he becomes more real, he manages somehow to project himself out of his imagined milieu, and, consequently, the world he inhabits, the frame, is suddenly transformed into a real world, very similar to that of Fielding

42

and his contemporaries. Whatever happens in the frame, then, is not only a reflection of what takes place in the London literary scene but also, with our willing suspension of disbelief, what *actually* occurs. The frame, in short, is not a representation of reality but reality itself; it is no longer a dramatic illusion, but a documentary of real events. Of course one might object that Fielding undermines the reality of his real characters when at the end of the play he breaks the frame and discovers unexpected relationships between his real characters and the less real puppets.[19] One could also argue that real people do not have names like Luckless, Mrs. Moneywood, Bookweight, and Witmore. Still, even with these objections, the effect Fielding creates by contrasting the real life of Harry Luckless with his artificial puppet show is to lend greater reality to the frame. This contrast, in turn, gives rise to the technique of double satire.

Double satire may be defined as the twofold censuring or ridiculing of an individual or subject matter, first in the frame, then in the puppet show. Like his creator, Luckless seems to fashion his satire out of his own unfortunate experience. That most incidents and characters are depicted twice also suggests that Fielding's farce violates the usual expectations of the mode, as enunciated by Gay and others, by being anything but incongruous and incoherent; the neat distribution of ten scenes for each of the first two acts, together with the presentation of climactic set pieces about the woes of writing at their respective centers, further reinforces the antifarcical structure of Fielding's farce. A few preliminary examples of correspondences between the two sections of the play suffice to establish its coherence. First, Charon's tart request for his "fare" from a penniless poet—"Never tell me, sir, I expect my fare" (p. 43)—echoes, in its language and intent, Mrs. Moneywood's opening salvo: "Never tell me, Mr. Luckless, of your play, and your play" (p. 7). Second, the matrimonial altercations between Punch and Joan recall the quarrels between Luckless and his cantankerous landlady, especially when these spats, because of the old matron's amorous designs on the young author, become parodies of marital discord. Finally, to reduce this catalogue to a manageable size, the operatic exchanges between Signior Opera and his paramours look back to the duets between Luckless and Harriot.

43

These parallels, however, are not strictly satirical in nature and therefore cannot be regarded as valid examples of double satire. Two characters in particular, both connected with the destruction of regular drama, receive this twofold satiric condemnation. Bookweight, presider over a garret full of impecunious scribblers who compose by committee and stale recipes, reappears as the Bookseller, whose name Curry intimates his kinship to Edmund Curll, that most unspeakable of mercenary publishers. Marplay, the interest-obsessed overseer of theatrical affairs, becomes Sir Farcical Comic, a more pointed delineation of Cibber, the original of both portraits.[20] These hits at well-known literary figures ground the satire in historical fact and contribute to its piquancy and urgency.[21] Even Hurlothrumbo, dismissed as a nonsensical play by Witmore, seeks a place in the court of the Goddess of Nonsense, much to Charon's elocutionary discomfort (p. 63). The rest of the "Persons in the Puppet Show"—a happily paradoxical collocation of words—do not have specific models in the frame, but represent concrete embodiments of the general dramatic maladies alluded to in the first two acts. By establishing in the frame that certain types of popular amusements and their perpetrators deserve to be ridiculed, Fielding differentiates Luckless's puppet show from the execrable entertainments it is meant to excoriate. The technique of double satire, then, acts as a distancing device to prevent confusion between the object of satiric scorn and its true-to-nature reflection in the satiric mirror.

Distancing devices, as one might expect, were crucial for writers in the insistently parodic scriblerian mode. When parody follows its original too closely, it risks being mistaken for what it is attacking. As William Shenstone wrote to the Reverend Richard Graves, "You cannot conceive how large the number is of those that mistake burlesque for the very foolishness it exposes (which observation I made once at the Rehearsal, at Tom Thumb, at Chrononhotonthologos all which are pieces of elegant humour)."[22] *Gulliver's Travels*, for instance, had achieved immense popularity largely because it had been read as the straightforward, highly amusing narrative of journeys into fantastic regions. In *Love in Several Masques*, Fielding remarks on this mindless reading or nonreading of Swift's work by having Lord Formal report Lady Rig's reaction to "that divine collection of polite learning written by Mr. Gulliver": "O the dear, sweet, pretty, little creatures! Oh, gemini! would I had been born a Lilliputian!" (3.10 [55]). Similarly, *The Beggar's Opera* enjoyed its vogue with the public because it satisfied their cravings for musical and visual extravaganzas. Scriblerus himself, in his Popean incarnation as commentator to *The Dunciad Variorum* (1729), is clearly a pedantic blockhead, until we examine the learned editions and pronouncements of Bentley, Burmann, Dennis, and Theobald, men who can be accused of all but mental feebleness, and realize that his brand of pedantry differs little from theirs. Despite their attempts to signal their intent by mock prefaces, footnotes, equivocations on textual reliability, and like distancing devices, Gay, Pope, and Swift were often misunderstood; the young Fielding, less confident perhaps about his artistic abilities and the purity of his motives, did not wish to meet the fate of his scriblerian forebears or, more pointedly, that of Luckless, who ends up being swallowed by his own artifice, as those presumably sturdy boundaries between art and life suddenly dissolve. Luckless's unexpected kinship to his puppets underscores how difficult it is for an author to extricate himself from his work, how chimerical his hope to escape responsibility for what he writes. Luckless begins as puppet master and, before he knows it, turns into a puppet. Fielding could not afford to make that mistake.

Indeed, the misunderstanding or misrepresentation of satiric purpose characterized the reception of the two plays that offered the main competition to *The Author's Farce* during its initial run; both plays were ballad operas in the "rehearsal" mode. Gabriel Odingsells' *Bays's Opera*, which opened at Drury Lane on 30 March and lasted only until the author's benefit on 1 April, featured dramatis personae similar to Fielding's: the author Bays (played by Theophilus Cibber), Cantato, "Usurper of the Empire of Wit," Pantomime, "Pretender to the Throne of Wit," Harlequin, "Chief Minister to Pantomime," and Farcia, "Pantomime's Daughter . . . a Libertine Coquette." As Odingsells ruefully confesses in his preface, the satiric intent of his "continu'd Allegory" was misunderstood: "The only view of this Performance was to expose the Folly and Absurdities of a prevailing (and, as I thought, vitiated) Taste; which seem'd to prefer Farce and Buffoonery, as well as the un-

45

profitable, immoral and unnatural Representations of Poetical Fiction, to the more polite and instructive Entertainments of Dramatick Poetry and Musick" (p. i).

The other piece, *The Fashionable Lady: or Harlequin's Opera,* James Ralph's first play, had a fairly successful run of eight performances at Goodman's Fields beginning on 2 April and was revived on 28 May to benefit Mrs. Mountfort; the performance of 17 June featured "An Epilogue by Penkethman riding on an Ass." In the *Grub-Street Journal* (23 April 1730), Bavius sardonically commends Ralph for his ineptitude as a dramatic satirist: "The farce now before me seems to have been written in imitation of the *Rehearsal*, and designed to ridicule the present fashionable entertainments. . . . Our author . . . contents himself with bantering them in the lump; and thinks it will be sufficient to turn the works of other men to ridicule, if he himself writes a very silly thing after the same manner. I entirely agree with him in this opinion; and if he will but oblige the town with a tragedy and a comedy of his composing; I do not at all question, but that both these species of poetry will be equally turned to ridicule." Similar charges would be leveled at Fielding throughout his dramatic career.

In addition to the technique of double satire, Fielding uses two other major distancing devices in *The Author's Farce:* Luckless as mediating authorial presence and the artificial, mechanical puppet show. Both devices have been the subject of recent critical discussion. Anthony J. Hassall, who has written on both, expresses the view, shared by J. Paul Hunter and C. J. Rawson among others, that the "authorial dimension" in the plays is a rudimentary adumbration of a technique Fielding would perfect in the novels.[23] This view, as I suggested earlier, has impeded our understanding of Fielding's accomplishment as a playwright. It is a hypothesis I shall endeavor to refute presently. Hassall has also offered an important assessment of Fielding's puppet show.[24] He concludes: "With characteristic irony [Fielding] took one of the humblest and least sophisticated forms of entertainment, and made it into an image of his own highly sophisticated art. . . . The structure of the puppet-show, with its master animating and manipulating his perennial figures, reconstructing his traditional story, and appearing before the curtain to mediate between stage and audience, is, in all

46

essentials, the structure of Fielding's novels and his most successful plays." With minor adjustments and elaborations, this might well be the definitive statement on this neglected but significant aspect of Fielding's art. My analysis of the puppet show in *The Author's Farce* takes Hassall's essay as its point of departure, as its main critical referent.

The central critical postulate about the authorial dimension in Fielding's plays has been that the technique is essentially nondramatic. In what stands, to date, as the most incisive treatment of Fielding's work in the theater, J. Paul Hunter has written:

> Fielding's plays do not prophesy that he will become a major novelist, but the direction of his theatrical career does suggest concerns that increasingly led him away from pure representation. He seems to be resisting the dramatic mode and moving toward forms that could more readily accommodate extreme degrees of artistic self-consciousness in its two main thrusts—concern with the process of creation and with the nature of response.
>
> Fielding's separation from the theatre was a forced one, but the expulsion was fortunate, freeing him from a relationship and commitment that had always been in some sense against the grain. His imagination, like that of many of his playwrights-within, often lacked metaphors for action. . . . Fielding's way is not really very dramatic, either in novels or in plays; he never developed stage-likely objective correlatives, having reserved his artistic energy for the examining process in which the action is rerun again and again, reviewed, considered, nearly masticated.[25]

It is strange that such a perceptive critic should feel that Fielding's method is undramatic. Hunter's peculiar position derives from his rather narrow conception of what constitutes the dramatic mode. For Hunter, that mode consists of "pure representation," of "metaphors for action," of "stage-likely objective correlatives." If Hunter is right, we must banish from the theater all those plays, in their most extreme forms usually mislabeled nonrepresentational, that do not adhere to the strict and unmediated depiction of believable characters interacting with one another through dialogue and action. We may call this the Aristotelian, or "negative capability," theory of drama, where the author is absent from his work and lets his characters do all the talking and all the acting. This, I should hasten to add, has been the traditional definition of drama, whose

47

general currency is attested to by the easy extensions of the word *dramatic* to other genres. A novelist, for example, is dramatic when he allows his characters to conduct themselves as they please, without his supervision. In this rather naive critical scheme—no writer can write and pretend that he is paring his fingernails—Richardson is a dramatic novelist and Fielding is not.[26] The view that dramatic novels are superior to those with authorial intrusions no longer commands the assent it once did; the house of fiction, critics recognize, has more than one room.[27] The belief that dramatic drama is somehow the only drama that can validly aspire to the name still needs to be combated.

The assumption that the authorial dimension in Fielding's plays is nondramatic stems, first of all, from the failure to grasp that these writers-within are, as C. J. Rawson has noted, "characters of the larger play we are watching, reduced to equal status with other characters."[28] Rawson's phrasing here is a bit misleading. Authors-within are indeed "characters of the larger play," but they are not "reduced." In fact, by standing at the front of the stage, between the audience and the internal play, they are, if anything, *magnified* and *separated*, both physically and mimetically, from the characters of the play-within. Rawson, however, makes this observation only as a disparaging aside, as another premise in his argument that Fielding does not manage his authorial intrusions in the plays as nicely as he does in the novels. But Rawson's point, even though he does not pursue it, is crucial. Once we learn to see the authorial presences *as parts of the plays* rather than as entities outside of them, we can begin to understand Fielding's method. Harry Luckless is, in many ways, a surrogate within the play for Harry Fielding. But before we start identifying him too closely with his creator, before we detach him from the play he is an integral part of, we must remember that he exists only *within* the play. Luckless, in other words, has no being except as a character in *The Author's Farce*. The possibility that Luckless can stand apart from the play in which he is a character can be entertained only by a reader, especially a reader familiar with Fielding's later novels. A spectator watching the play cannot separate the two: he does not see Luckless *and The Author's Farce*, but Luckless *within The Author's Farce*. We simply cannot dismember a work of art to suit our generic precon-

Defending authorial intrusion in the play

ceptions—or, in this case, misconceptions. An authorial presence, then, is not incompatible with the dramatic mode; the two are not mutually exclusive phenomena. In *The Author's Farce* and his other irregular plays, with the important exception of *The Tragedy of Tragedies* (1731), Fielding combines these two supposedly antithetical elements—which, in the last analysis, cannot be spoken of as discrete units, since one contains the other—to fashion a different, though by no means entirely new, dramatic form.

The claim that the authorial dimension is nondramatic becomes even less tenable when one recognizes the technique's ancient and venerable pedigree, from the choruses in Greek tragedy and comedy, particularly in Euripides (significantly, Aristotle's least favorite tragedian) and Aristophanes, through the playwrights-within of the Elizabethan stage, most notably Hamlet, the inventor of the "mousetrap," to the plotters and mar-plotters of seventeenth-century drama. During the Restoration and the eighteenth century, this internal authorial persona grew into the dominant feature of a certain type of satiric play, defined for the period by *The Rehearsal* (1671) of Buckingham, Butler, and others, itself an imitation of Molière's *L'Impromptu de Versailles* and, to a lesser extent, of Davenant's *The Play-House to be Lett*, both performed in 1663.[29] Buckingham's piece was revived virtually every season after 1671, with the identity of Bayes, originally intended as a dig at Dryden, constantly changing to accommodate the latest theatrical bête noire. By 1730, then, the rehearsal form, with its prominent authorial dimension, provided the most obvious vehicle for the dissection of corrupt dramatic practices. Fielding's adaptation of the form should surprise no one conversant with contemporary theatrical conventions: the authorial dimension was sanctioned by the best dramatic authorities.

The authorial dimension can be defended as a valid dramatic technique, finally, by reference to the aims and emphases of the plays in which it is employed. If traditional drama strives, at least in theory, to present a faithful picture of reality, to hold a mirror up to nature, Fielding's irregular plays are decidedly unnatural, artificial, and, in this sense at least, non-Aristotelian. For Aristotle, tragedy imitates a natural action, and brings about a catharsis, or purgation, by engaging the passions of the audience, by eliciting an

49

emotional identification with the characters on stage, an identification made possible by the fidelity of the mimetic representation.[30] Fielding, on the other hand, seeks to distance his viewers from the action he is representing. Fielding's representation is still mimetic in that it imitates the form of certain popular amusements, but his satiric purpose would be defeated if his audience were to sympathize with the happenings unfolding before them, if they were to mistake the explosion of the pleasures of the town for the pleasures themselves. For this reason he needs to make his spectators view these occurrences from a detached perspective, not a sympathetic one. As Brecht would do two centuries later in his epic theatre by relying on masks, signs, stylized acting, and other illusion-shattering techniques, Fielding aims for an intellectual response by preventing close emotional involvement with his play.[31]

Desire to
prevent
close
emotional
involvement

Fielding, as suggested above, begins *The Author's Farce* as a conventional romantic comedy and, as a result of this initial procedure, invites the traditional Aristotelian identification with his hero. Once he has manipulated his audience into experiencing this identification, however, he forces them to change their point of view, to rethink their preconceptions about theatrical illusion. As readers or spectators we never lose our interest in Luckless's fortunes, in fact may even be delighted by his ludicrous restoration to the Bantamite throne because of its perverse fulfillment of our initial generic expectations of poetic justice. But when he stands between us and the puppet show and explicitly announces his satiric intent to the player (p. 39), we cannot identify with his play. The artificiality of the puppet show may make Luckless seem more real, but the reverse is also true. His fictional being, his status as a character within the play, relegates his creation to an even higher (or lower) realm of artifice. Fielding's manipulation of our responses, the contrast he effects between our initial identification with Luckless and our subsequent detachment from his puppet show, explains his use of the author-within in purely dramatic terms. Thus the authorial dimension in Fielding's plays is not an undramatic lapse symptomatic of his inability to attain pure representation but a dramatic technique wholly justified, indeed demanded, by the aims and emphases of his intellectual theater. Luckless's insistent presence and intrusions as puppet master do not allow us to take his puppets for anything but *his* puppets, or to interpret his creator's imitations of current spectacles as anything but Fielding's revenge on those who sought to destroy the theater, a revenge carried out, most fittingly, by appropriating their very own implements of destruction.[32]

One of these implements was, of course, the puppet show. Because of Hassall's magisterial essay on the subject and what has already been said about puppets in the preceding pages, we need not devote much time to this device. Yet Hassall seems to me to stress too vehemently the paradigmatic nature of Fielding's use of the puppet image and to lessen its importance as a debased species of entertainment. To be sure, Hassall admits that the puppet show was a low form, but he then moves too quickly to assertions about Fielding's artistic transformations of it. As Hassall puts it, the "happiest irony [of the puppet show] is that in using a low form to satirize the low taste of the age, Fielding had stooped only to conquer."[33] This observation, needless to say, is corroborated by my own analysis and reading of the play. But I place more emphasis on the stooping than the conquering. When Fielding began composing *The Author's Farce*, he did not intend to present the puppet show as an image of his dramatic and novelistic art. Instead, as the prologue to the play and Luckless's words to the player make clear, he meant to use the puppet show as another satiric barb at his opponents precisely because he considered the form to be "low" and "beneath the dignity of the stage" (p. 39). Moreover, "farces" and "puppet shows," so inextricably fused in this play that one cannot speak of one without implying the other, were popular with contemporary audiences. And for an impecunious author the emptiness of his purse and belly acts as a stronger incentive than artistic integrity. In Luckless's words: "Who would not then rather eat by his nonsense than starve by his wit?" (p. 39). Or, as Samuel Johnson, the more famous namesake of the mad dancing master from Cheshire, phrased this eternal verity of a writer's life: "No man but a blockhead ever wrote, except for money."[34]

Fielding was no blockhead, and in 1730, as his prospects in regular drama appeared to have darkened, he desperately needed to find a way to make that money. In this respect Luckless's final coronation as the ruler of the fabulously rich kingdom of Bantam represents Fielding's wish-fulfillment of his own longing for fame and wealth, a longing that would be satisfied in the real world by the immense success of *The Author's Farce*. And *The Author's Farce* would succeed because of Fielding's willingness to accommodate his art, as Cibber claimed to have done in *The Provok'd Husband*, and give the public what it wanted. In so doing, he would also begin to define his aims and methods as a playwright, to find his own dramatic voice.

The Life and Critical Opinions of H. Scriblerus Secundus: *Tom Thumb* and *The Tragedy of Tragedies*

ON 24 April 1730, the ninth night of its opening run, *The Author's Farce* was performed with a new afterpiece, *Tom Thumb. A Tragedy.* Whether Fielding's first irregular drama would have achieved its great popularity without this addition is difficult to ascertain; what is certainly beyond dispute is that, as parts of the same bill, both plays delighted audiences at the Haymarket for over thirty nights, until 22 June, when they yielded the stage to the prolific young dramatist's next attempt at regular comedy, *Rape upon Rape;* and the two plays were paired off once again on 3 July, a one-night revival that ended the most successful theatrical partnership of the year. *Tom Thumb*, for its part, continued to be acted throughout the summer, most notably with *Rape upon Rape* on 1 July; and, as proof of its appeal beyond the walls of the Little Theatre, it was offered by the Haymarket company, after the conclusion of the season, at Bartholomew Fair on 4 September and at Southwark Fair on 14 September.[1]

These several appearances of *Tom Thumb* without *The Author's Farce*, as well as its subsequent transformation into the longer, more magnificent *Tragedy of Tragedies*, have obscured the obvious yet crucial fact that the little play began its illustrious career as the afterpiece to *The Author's Farce*, a fact so obvious that it has eluded critical notice, as has *Tom Thumb* itself. Critics of the play, from James T. Hillhouse onward, have chosen to focus on *The Tragedy of*

Tragedies and to ignore its seemingly insubstantial first version. This is a regrettable oversight because *Tom Thumb* constitutes a vital link in Fielding's dramatic career, its importance lying not so much in its later expansion into scriblerian complexity as in its debt to, and departure from, the play it followed on stage for thirty-three nights in 1730. To arrive at a more balanced critical assessment of *Tom Thumb*, we must begin by exploring its origins in *The Author's Farce*; only then can we analyze the nexus between *Tom Thumb* and *The Tragedy of Tragedies*. Both connections must be examined to appreciate more fully the evolution of Fielding's thought about the theater.

Tom Thumb narrows the general satire of *The Author's Farce* by concentrating on one particularly risible pleasure of the town, that species of cliché-ridden heroic tragedy which, though full of sound and fury, signifies absolutely nothing. As the second interlude of Luckless's puppet show begins, the Goddess of Nonsense enjoins her "votaries" to "prepare / To celebrate this joyful day," on which she will choose a mate from among her many suitors, each of whom represents a contemporary popular amusement.[2] Don Tragedio is one of these, but he must share the limelight with such eminent dunces as Dr. Orator, Sir Farcical, Monsieur Pantomime, and Signior Opera. He is one among many, one contributor to the demise of common sense in the playhouse, but no more or less notorious than the rest. What Fielding is underscoring here, by this method of guilt by association or propinquity, is the pervasiveness of the malady, the interchangeableness of the pretenders to the hand of the empty-headed divinity—the difficulty, in short, of drawing boundaries, of determining where one abuse ends and the next one begins. In its attempt at comprehensiveness, Luckless's puppet show thus runs the risk of diffusiveness, a diffusiveness that threatens its satiric effectiveness. As one purveyor of nonsense follows another, with no apparent sequence or purpose, the spectator soon realizes that the series could be extended into infinity; the only way the puppet show can end is by the intervention of characters from the frame. Nonsense tends to run away with itself, but satire must be more controlled, must have a clearer object of attack, to achieve its purpose. *Tom Thumb* sharpens the focus of Fielding's satire on

54

the pleasures of the town by drawing boundaries, by giving all these general and protean entities a definite name and habitation.

Tom Thumb, then, takes one episode from *The Author's Farce* and expands it into a close study of one particular manifestation of theatrical nonsense. *Tom Thumb* is, in other words, the type of tragedy Don Tragedio would write, and, as a result, it derives its principal characteristics from those tenets the worthy tragedian identifies as the most salient of his aesthetic creed: his ignorance of, and disregard for, the dramatic tradition ("To Shakespeare, Jonson, Dryden, Lee, or Rowe / I not a line, no, not a thought do owe"), which account, in turn, for his "novelty" because, as he explains, "as I wrote none ever wrote before." This novelty in composition, as Luckless helpfully points out, gives rise to "another excellence of the Don's": his ability to use language with strikingly bathetic originality by making up "new bad words of his own," such as the decidedly untragic "by jay'd" (p. 54). For, like Bayes in *The Rehearsal*, Don Tragedio is an advocate and practitioner of the "new Wit." When Johnson and Smith ask Bayes why he has written a play about *two* kings of Brentford, the learned author haughtily replies, "Because it's new; and that's it I aim at. I despise your *Johnson* and *Beaumont*, that borrow'd all they writ from Nature: I am for fetching it purely out of my own fancy, I" and, like his Fieldingesque descendant, Bayes affects a "stile" that "was never yet upon the Stage."[3] It is one of Fielding's most delicious ironies that a character so disdainful of tradition as Don Tragedio should owe his being, his very words and attitudes, to a dramatic antecedent.[4]

Don Tragedio's use of language without regard to tradition, nature, or sense represents, then, his main contribution to the decline of the dramatic genre he embodies. But if this is his main contribution, the best argument he can advance for his merit as the future husband of the Goddess of Nonsense, he soon finds out that he is not alone—to borrow a turn from Cibberian, or "prefatical," speech—in excelling at this "excellence." Sir Farcical, for example, can match and top the Don's claims to linguistic originality: "I have made new words, and spoiled old ones too. . . . I have made foreigners break English and Englishmen break Latin. I have as great a confusion of languages in my play as was at the building of Babel" (p. 55). And so can Dr. Orator. Indeed, with the possible exception of Monsieur Pantomime, who sins against language only by his inability to speak, every character in Luckless's puppet show is guilty of verbal misconduct. The poor Poet, for instance, who humbly professes an acquaintance with the muses, easily sinks into the "Profund of *Scriblerus*" (preface to *Tom Thumb*, p. 17) when describing the goddess's reaction to the amatory warblings of Signior Opera: "I saw her like another Dido. I saw her heart rise up to her eyes, and drop down again to her ears" (*The Author's Farce*, p. 48). With friends like this, the muses need few enemies. For the truth is that nobody in Luckless's literary underworld can escape the contagion, even those with the best intentions; the contempt for language, in short, is the bond that holds all the "Persons in the Puppet Show" together in the same play. In *Tom Thumb* Fielding isolates this central thematic concern of *The Author's Farce* and explores it at length in one of its most prominent and sonorous incarnations.

But as soon as Fielding decides to focus on only one of the many pleasures of the town, he discovers that what makes "modern Tragedy" so ridiculous and dramatically inept is that it has ceased to be pure tragedy and become mixed with "farce," that the modern failure to observe generic boundaries still lies at the root of the problem.[5] Contemporary tragedians write farcical tragedies because, like Bayes and Don Tragedio, they have lost sight of the tragic tradition, either through straining after fantastical ways of making it new or through unimaginative variations of the old. A playwright can miss the mark either by flouting tradition and decorum or by being a slave to them; both procedures bespeak an improper relation to his models. Rather, he must recognize when a dramatic form has become exhausted, when the tradition needs to be revitalized with new ideas, while realizing at the same time, that this revitalization, this introduction of the new, must be carried out judiciously, with due respect toward the old. A dramatist with no sense of the past, with no judgment to discern when a change is needed or the skill to implement it, is bound to engage in farcical distortions of the tradition. If he is a tragedian, he will unwittingly join "the Sock to the Buskin," and write what Fielding oxymoron-

56

ically calls "laughing" tragedies.[6] *Tom Thumb* differs from other "laughing" tragedies in the intentionality of its laughter.

The link between *The Author's Farce* and *Tom Thumb* is, therefore, not only one of simple chronological sequence, of main piece to afterpiece, but also one of genre: both are farces, in the special Fielding sense of farce as the peculiarly modern guise of the more traditional, more legitimate dramatic genres of comedy and tragedy. Equally as important as these similarities are the differences between the two plays, the most significant of which is clearly that of dramatic presentation. *The Author's Farce*, as I argued in my last chapter, relies on a series of distancing devices to prevent the spectator from confusing the satiric explosion of the pleasures of the town with the pleasures themselves. The frame provided by the life of Harry Luckless, the puppet show with its mechanical acting, Luckless as controlling and commenting puppet master—all these do not allow the audience to identify with the spectacle on stage, to take it straight, as it were. Like the outer play in *The Rehearsal*, which clearly singles out the inner play as a worthy object of scorn, these devices in *The Author's Farce* point toward and frame the satiric object.

In *Tom Thumb* Fielding plays a more dangerous game, though the first appearance of the play ensured, to a large extent, that its satiric purpose would not be missed. An audience that just watched *The Author's Farce* is not likely to misinterpret the aim of *Tom Thumb*. But as soon as the play began to appear by itself, with its satiric umbilical cord severed, so to speak, it had to convey its intent unaided. Fielding had of course provided for this eventuality, as we shall see, in the very language and structure of the work, despite his continued diffidence about the effectiveness and unequivocalness of his new method, as evinced by his scriblerian addition of prologues, prefaces, and footnotes to the play, beginning with its second printed edition. But these came later and belong to the machinery whereby *Tom Thumb* was gradually metamorphosed from an acting into a reading play. The acting *Tom Thumb*—or, for that matter, the acting *Tragedy of Tragedies*—differs from both *The Author's Farce* and *The Rehearsal* in completing the inner play, in giving full autonomy to the satiric object. Once Fielding decided to dispense with the rehearsal structure in *Tom Thumb*, however, he had to find other means to convey his satiric intentions; the frameless inner play had to contain the seeds of its own satiric destruction.

Fielding did not have to search long for a new dramatic method. Given the inherent absurdities of "modern Tragedy," the form had already become, in many ways, a parody of itself, as men as diverse in their critical sensibilities as Addison, Buckingham, Dennis, and Pope had pointed out. Viewed from this perspective, *Tom Thumb* is almost an exercise in the art of redundancy. All Fielding had to do was to take the basic elements of contemporary tragedy as he would have found them displayed in Don Tragedio's words "at Lincoln's Inn and eke at Drury Lane" (*The Author's Farce*, p. 54) and give them a slight rhetorical push to reveal their underlying inanities, a method of satiric reductio ad absurdum similar to that he was to use with uproarious results a decade later in *Shamela*, his burlesque of Richardson's sanctimonious *Pamela* (1740). In this respect *Tom Thumb* may be seen as Fielding's deconstructive commentary on "modern Tragedy" because, like the deconstructive critic, Fielding exposes "the element in the system . . . which is alogical, the thread . . . which will unravel it all . . . the loose stone which will pull down the whole building." Fielding's dramatic method in *Tom Thumb* resembles deconstruction in that—to adapt the words of J. Hillis Miller—it "is not a dismantling of the structure" of heroic tragedy so much as a "demonstration" that the genre "has already dismantled itself."[7] Although Miller's description of deconstruction focuses on only one aspect of Derrida's critique of discourse, thereby reducing a complex philosophical procedure to a clever linguistic game, it nonetheless serves my purpose here by offering an analogy, in the language of current critical discourse, to Fielding's parodic techniques in *Tom Thumb*. Fielding shares the deconstructive critic's joy in revealing the undermining duplicity of (in this case) the language and conventions of heroic tragedy. But unlike the deconstructive critic, Fielding wishes to arrest the process of deconstruction, which, if relentlessly pursued and applied—or, in heroic tragedy, if allowed to continue to pursue its own self-undermining tendencies—will inevitably end in nothingness. The basic assumptions and procedures of what Derrida and his followers have called deconstruction were not wholly unknown to Fielding, though he would have given them the more familiar appellation of scriblerian satire.

To achieve its satiric purpose, however, scriblerian satire must not only identify "the loose stone which will pull down the whole building" but also dislodge it to make sure that the building will actually collapse. Wretched as "modern Tragedy" was, it remained immensely popular, popular enough to survive the constant castigations of many a self-appointed arbiter of theatrical taste. For example, Charles Gildon, in *The Laws of Poetry* (1721), advances that while Dryden might have been justified in the characterization of his heroes—"at the time when those characters were form'd, bullying was altogether the mode, off the stage, as well as upon it"—"that humour is since much abated in the conversation of the world." Yet, he adds, "there remains so far a relish for it, that to this day an audience is never so well pleas'd as when an actor foams with some extravagant rant" (p. 350). In Gildon's view even Shakespeare has been guilty of perpetrating the "fantastic gallimaufry" called "modern Tragedy" (p. 149). He praises both *The Rehearsal* and Thomas Rymer for exposing the "monstrous absurdities which . . . were applauded . . . as excellencies" during the reign of Charles II: "What fantastical and ridiculous pieces those were, which even to our days bear the name of the best *Tragic* performances in our language, I mean *The Maid's Tragedy; King, and no King;* Rollo, *Duke* of Normandy. . . . The charge Mr. *Rymer* brings against these plays is, that they have no *Fable*, and by consequence can give no instruction; that their *manners* and *sentiments*, to say nothing of the *diction*, are every where defective, nay unnatural, and therefore can give no rational or useful pleasure" (pp. 156–57). That "modern Tragedy" was nothing more than a collection of clichés is stressed in the advice offered in the *Universal Spectator*, no. 218 (9 December 1732), to "a young Gentleman preparing to write a *Tragedy*": "The present Method may be drawn into the following general *Receipt.*—Take a *Love Story,* add thereto an immensurable Length of Time, Characters undistinguish'd by anything but the Names; *Scenes* here, there, and everywhere, *Entrances* and *Exits* without Occasion, *Descriptions* for the Sake of the Verses, *Soliloquies* to shew how well we can argue, and *Asides* because its the Fashion; *Murders* without Reason,

59

and *Punishments* without *Justice*, not forgetting a *Simile* in Rhime at the End of every Act."

Under these circumstances, Fielding could not merely duplicate a "modern Tragedy" and let it go at that. Had he done so, his audience would have seen his duplication as yet another example of the genre and would have reacted accordingly. However bad these plays were, they were still recognized as tragedies because of their adherence to certain conventions which the public through long exposure to them had thoroughly internalized and therefore tacitly accepted as legitimately tragic. Once these plays were accepted as legitimately tragic, they could then command the traditional suspension of disbelief which, in a theater governed by Aristotelian precept and assumptions, as was the theater of Fielding's day, invariably leads to the spectator's identification with the action unfolding on stage. And, as Fielding well understood, it is virtually impossible to grasp the absurdity of something we sympathize or identify with, especially at the very moment we are completely caught up in the theatrical illusion during a dramatic performance.[8] He thus set out to prevent this identification by disrupting the theatrical illusion; and he would cause this disruption by presenting the conventions of "modern Tragedy" in a disconcertingly new context.

When Fielding removes the conventions of "modern Tragedy" from their serious context and places them, through a process of reduction and inversion, in a comically absurd framework in *Tom Thumb*, he is simply carrying to its logical conclusion the alogical dissociation of tragic meaning from tragic structure in the genre. That is, he merely widens the fissure that already exists in contemporary tragedy between its form and its potentially laughable dramatic situations; and he actualizes that potentiality by creating a more obvious discontinuity between content and form, between the tragic conventions and their untragic surroundings, by introducing, as it were, a dissonant note into the apparently harmonious music of "modern Tragedy." Like the "one discordant Word [that] spoils the whole Sentence, and makes it entirely Prefatical,"[9] Fielding's subversive collocation of ludicrous subject matter and tragic conventions in *Tom Thumb* fractures the faulty syntax of contem-

60

porary heroic tragedy and exposes the hidden laughter beneath its
familiar solemnities.

Tom Thumb, as J. Paul Hunter has noted, "depends primarily
on one joke," on the Lilliputian size of its "great" hero.[10] Nearly
twenty years earlier, Addison had deplored the facile equation between physical and spiritual attributes in contemporary performances of heroic tragedy: "The ordinary Method of making an
Heroe, is to clap a huge Plume of Feathers upon his Head, which
rises so very high, that there is often a greater Length from his Chin
to the Top of his Head, than to the Sole of his Foot. One could
believe, that we thought a great Man and a tall Man the same
Thing."[11] Fielding undermines this absurd equation by making his
hero a "little insignificant Fellow" (*Tom Thumb*, p. 31), whose dim-
inutive size, as other characters around him continually stress, is so
strangely at odds with the magnitude of his purported accomplishments that Grizzle, for one, doubts their veracity and believes them
the result of a "Trick" (p. 27). Grizzle, of course, has an ax to grind
here, since he is the little hero's rival at court, but his point is well
taken. The disparity between the hero's greatness and size thus
becomes a striking theatrical metaphor that draws its satiric power
from the tension between unheroic vehicle and supposedly heroic
tenor, a tension that would have been delightfully heightened when
a woman played the part during the original run of the play and
the hero became not only a midget but a transvestite as well. Inversion, in *Tom Thumb*, affects more than the physical stature of the
protagonist.

If Tom Thumb has problems filling his heroic role because of
his small dimensions and tantalizingly ambiguous sexuality,[12] he is
equally helpless when it comes to justifying his merit as a tragic
hero by reference to a noble birth. A tragic hero needs to be of
lofty lineage, yet Tom Thumb is reputed to have been hatched
from a "Pudding."[13] Unlike most of his colleagues at Drury Lane
and Lincoln's Inn, he owes his literary origins to popular English
legend, not to classical history or mythology, as Fielding perhaps
obeys, with tongue far into his cheek, Addison's injunctions to
British writers to eschew pagan sources and choose models of a
more native stamp, such as the ballad of Chevy Chase which the

Spectator, in his seventieth and seventy-fourth papers, claims to find vastly superior to many a classical parallel.[14] This tragically inappropriate choice of subject the author defends as his "chief Merit," presumably because it does not reveal the split between subject matter and form in contemporary tragedy as much as the selection of classical material would. A debased genre, in other words, ought to deal with a debased topic: "modern Tragedy" deserves to have a suitably modern hero. As Scriblerus Secundus writes in his preface to the play: "It is with great Concern that I have observed several of our (the *Grubstreet*) Tragical Writers, to Celebrate in their Immortal Lines the Actions of Heroes recorded in Historians and Poets, such as *Homer* or *Virgil*, *Livy* or *Plutarch*, the Propagation of whose Works is so apparently against the Interest of our Society; when the Romances, Novels, and Histories, *vulgo* call'd Story-Books, of our own People, furnish such abundant and proper Themes for their Pens, such are *Tom Tram*, *Hickathrift*, &c." (p. 18). In this sense *Tom Thumb* is the first tragedy to recognize its own limitations, the first example of a new species of Grub Street tragedy, humble (if not low) in its origins, subject matter, and execution: the first work, that is, to exploit fully the manifold scriptorial "excellences" of modern tragedians, excellences hitherto wasted on grossly uncongenial dramatic subjects and situations. We can examine a few of the more exquisite "excellences" of Fielding's laughing tragedy.

Tom Thumb depicts that one "auspicious Day" on which, as Doodle tells Noodle in a typically maladroit simile and personification, the sun "shines like a Beau in a new Birth-Day Suit" and "all Nature . . . grins for Joy" and on which, as Noodle tells Doodle in equally exalted strains, "the mighty *Thomas Thumb* victorious comes" to Arthur's court to lead in triumph the giants he has conquered: "So some Cock-Sparrow in a Farmer's Yard, / Hops at the Head of an huge Flock of Turkeys" (p. 23). As a reward for the little warrior's valorous deeds, the king promises to give him in marriage his amply endowed daughter, the peerless Huncamunca. This act of royal generosity arouses the wrath and jealousy of the queen and Grizzle, who conspire to prevent the intended nuptials. "This Day," as Noodle acutely and tautologically observes, "is a Day / Indeed, a Day we never saw before"—that day, in short,

62

during which, according to such neoclassical interpreters of Aristotle's pronouncements on the dramatic unities as Scriblerus (who cites Corneille as his authority), a tragic action must unfold, a day that recalls, among other things, that "joyful day" in Luckless's puppet show when the Goddess of Nonsense chooses a companion.[15] It is also the day that will sadly witness the protagonist's ignominious and dramatically illogical double death as he is first swallowed by a cow and then, as Fielding facetiously illustrates the Aristotelian principle of character conservation, has his ghost slain by the envious Grizzle, a feat so absurd that it is reported to have made Swift laugh aloud for only the second time in his life.[16]

The improbable drama of Tom Thumb's brief day in the sun was no doubt acted with all the farcical gusto, all the horseplay and slapstick, the Haymarket company could muster, so that the dean's mirth would have been aroused not only by the ludicrous metaphor at work in the last scene of the tragedy—captured in "several celebrated Plays," as the literal-minded Scriblerus adduces in answer to "*Kriticks*" of his ending, in "such Expressions as these, *Kill my Soul, Stab my very Soul . . . cum multis aliis*, all which visibly confess that for a Soul or Ghost to be killed is no Impossibility" (p. 18)— but also by having that metaphor fleshed out and performed before him (note Scriblerus's telling adverb "visibly") with all due grimaces and exaggerated gestures. Those original performances, unfortunately, must remain for us a matter of conjecture and imaginative projection. What we have instead is the script, the reading play, and it is written in that miraculous dialect which Scriblerus, as he gropes for words to express his admiration, ventures "to call the Supernatural, after the celebrated Author of *Hurlothrumbo*" (p. 17). That "Supernatural" language, most readers agree, is the crowning excellence of *Tom Thumb*, from which all other excellences draw their being.

Although Scriblerus specifically identifies the "Supernatural" as the essence of "prefatical" language, it is clear that part of his definition can be extended to account for the linguistic peculiarities of the play itself. In order for a word to "enter into a Preface," Scriblerus expounds, it must be "stripped of all its Ideas," which can be done either by "adding, diminishing, or changing a Letter, as instead of Paraphernalia, writing *Paraphonalia*" or by "putting half a dozen incoherent [words] together: Such as *when the People of our Age shall be Ancestors*, &c." (ibid.), both direct hits at Cibber's fanciful lingo in his address to the reader of *The Provok'd Husband*, as Fielding continues the attack he had begun in *The Author's Farce* on his famous contemporary's farcical renderings of the English tongue. These two Cibberian methods of stripping words of ideas, but especially the second, help to explain the verbal vacuity of *Tom Thumb:* only a language devoid of all thought can be molded with such ease into the empty sonorities uttered by virtually every character in the play.

similes

The linguistic aphasia that this "Supernatural" language engenders in its speakers is nowhere more evident than in their inability to create effective similes. A simile connects two separate realms of experience by identifying one or more points of similarity between them, with its success being measured both by the novelty and the appropriateness of the similitude. The best simile is one that has never been made before, but, once made, strikes the judicious reader or auditor as just right, as most natural and precise. Only the most discerning of artists and speakers can fashion a good simile; only a language capable of making accurate connections can produce a fitting comparison. The speaker of a language that has severed all ties between its words and ideas, between its verbal signs and their referents in the universe at large, cannot grasp the adequacy or inadequacy of a simile because his language has no memory, no standard by which to judge. As a result, when he strives for new comparisons, he either repeats old similes because he cannot recall their previous appearances in the literary tradition or makes outlandish connections because his language is not equipped to discriminate between contexts or styles. High and low, the vulgar and the elegant, the bombastic and the sublime—all these have no meaning in a language that is not aware of itself, of its history, or of the milieu in which it is spoken. We laugh at the ensuing linguistic anarchy because our language, unlike that of the characters in *Tom Thumb*, still retains some semblance of order and organization. We see the absurdity of these similes because we remember other similes that do not violate decorum and because we still inhabit a world where "an huge Flock of Turkeys" cannot function as a suitable analogy for an army of defeated giants—at least

64

not in a literary work that aspires to be taken seriously. Similes in *Tom Thumb*, then, reflect the discontinuities of "modern Tragedy" by juxtaposing tenors and vehicles that can be joined only by the most perverse linguistic will, by minds that have renounced logic and syntax, by characters who have forgotten the meaningful correspondences between language and reality.

Noodle and Doodle are, of course, not the only characters in *Tom Thumb* who boggle our minds with their Cibberian rhetoric nor is the botched simile the play's only weapon against the English language. Scriblerus's arsenal of "Supernatural" ammunition is, in fact, so well stocked that it precludes full documentation.[17] A few examples must suffice, therefore, to establish what cannot be wholly substantiated without quoting both *Tom Thumb* and *The Tragedy of Tragedies* in their entirety. No wonder we are relieved when in *The Tragedy of Tragedies* the tiny hero, upon being asked by the king to describe what giants look like, succinctly replies, "Like Nothing but Themselves" (p. 55). We are particularly relieved if we remember that in *Tom Thumb* he had answered the same query with

> Like twenty Things, my Liege;
> Like twenty thousand Oaks, by Winter's Hand
> Strip'd of their Blossoms; like a Range of Houses,
> When Fire has burnt their Timber all away.
>
> (p. 25)

Although his brief rejoinder in the second play may be interpreted, if we wish to be ingenious, as his dim awareness of the inability of his self-referential language to construct valid similes or even perhaps as his punning admission of the unsubstantiality or nothingness of the giants, it offers on a more practical level a welcome respite to ears abused by *Tom Thumb* and about to be assaulted by the bathetic verbal salvos of the remaining scenes of *The Tragedy of Tragedies*. Tom Thumb's firm rejection of the king's invitation to murder the English language, his momentary refusal to participate in the linguistic chaos of Arthur's court, represents his most heroic deed; no other character, with the possible exception of the king himself, evinces such courage and good sense in either version of the play.

The king's impatience with verbal ineptitude arises, however, more out of his irascibility (exacerbated, no doubt, by drink) than out of his innate aesthetic sensibility. When Noodle, for example, bemoans the death of Tom Thumb with the bombastic

> Oh monstrous! dreadful! terrible! Oh! Oh!
> Deaf be my Ears, for ever blind my Eyes,
> Dumb be my Tongue, Feet lame, all Senses lost

—a passage which, incidentally, comments on its own rhetorical clumsiness by calling attention both to its loss of sense and to its metrical lameness—the king replies with a terse "What does the Blockhead mean?" (p. 37). And when, in *The Tragedy of Tragedies*, the ghost of Gaffer Thumb concludes his dire prophecies with a long string of "So have I seens," the irate monarch unceremoniously interrupts him with "D—n all thou'st seen!" (p. 86)—an outburst that culminates in his subsequent soliloquy with a blast against all makers of similes:

> Curst be the Man who first a Simile made!
> Curst, ev'ry Bard who writes!—So have I seen
> Those whose Comparisons are just and true,
> And those who liken things not like at all.
> The Devil is happy, that the whole Creation
> Can furnish out no Simile to his Fortune.
>
> (p. 87)

By thus recruiting the king as an unwitting ally in his war on "Verba Tragica" (p. 76), Fielding achieves an effect reminiscent of that attained by Chaucer in *The Canterbury Tales* when he lets his otherwise unperceptive "Hoost" put an end to the agonizing tale of Sir Thopas with the abrupt "Namoore of this, for Goddes dignitee" and the apt critical assessment, "Thy drasty ryming is nat worth a toord!"[18] In this fashion, the two authors hope not only to render more explicit what should have dawned on the reader or spectator long before this point in the action—if the host and the king can notice the blunder, it must be really bad—but also to dissociate themselves even further from any complicity in the linguistic chaos they are so faithfully reproducing. This unexpected comment from within the text is, in short, another one of Fielding's distancing devices, his way of signaling, as bluntly as he can, his

66

satiric intention to those of us with less than agile intellects, but particularly to those of his contemporaries who, he rightly feared, would cite *Tom Thumb* as incontrovertible evidence for the decline of English drama.[19]

Despite its "Supernatural" foundations, the language of *Tom Thumb* is not so chaotic as to be utterly disjointed and unintelligible; indeed, there are times when its peculiar effects stem not so much from its failure to make appropriate connections between words and ideas as from its grim determination to pursue relations or analogies so ludicrously obvious or inconsequential that only a demented logician would care to follow them to their inevitable conclusions. Such, for example, is the case when the king extends the queen's cliché—"Excess of Joy, my Lord, I've heard Folks say, / Gives Tears, as often as Excess of Grief"—into an apocalyptic vision of lachrymal destruction for his kingdom:

If it be so, let all Men cry for Joy,
'Till the whole Court be drowned with their Tears;
Nay, 'till they overflow my utmost Land,
And leave me nothing but the Sea to rule.

(p. 24)

Or, to cite another instance, when Grizzle, enraged by the queen's calling him a "Setting-Dog," spins out a simile almost canine in the way it chases its own rhetorical tail:

So when two Dogs are fighting in the Streets,
With a third Dog, one of the two Dogs meets,
With angry Teeth, he bites him to the Bone,
And this Dog smarts for what that Dog had done.

(pp. 27–28)

It is not simply that the king has neglected to ponder the real consequences for his land and subjects of the deluge he so merrily conjures up or that Grizzle can see neither the inadequacy of the queen's analogy nor the extent to which he confirms his sovereign's unregal epithet by accepting and expanding its figurative premise, but that both characters cannot recognize those boundaries because their language does not allow them to remember that such boundaries exist, that a cliché is such a fragile entity that it cannot be looked at too closely without uncovering its essential triviality and absurdity,[20] that a metaphor cannot be "*run . . . down*, and pursue[d] . . . as far as it can go," as Pope's Scriblerus encourages his fellow students of the "Abuse of Speech" to do in *Peri Bathous*, without upsetting its delicate balance.[21] The king and Grizzle cannot leave bad enough alone; their language dies of its own too much.

Another way to expose the absurdity of a cliché or hackneyed metaphor is to attempt to visualize it. When the queen realizes that she "can't live / Without [her] Virtue, or without *Tom Thumb*," she decides to "weigh them in two equal Scales": "In this Scale put my Virtue, that, *Tom Thumb*. / Alas! *Tom Thumb* is heavier than my Virtue" (p. 28). Our pleasure in this inanity, while no doubt enhanced by our recollection of its Homeric prototype in the twenty-second book of the *Iliad*,[22] derives primarily from the queen's literal-mindedness, from her inability, on the one hand, to distinguish between her abstract virtue and the fleshly—and, to follow her logic, understandably heavier—Tom Thumb; and from her failure, on the other hand, to discriminate between figurative speech and the real objects and actions which those figures once described and which they have now displaced. Her language, with no memory to guide it, must of necessity recreate the origins of its metaphors and clichés because it cannot prevent its speakers from attempting to reify what custom has transformed into an abstract rhetorical device. The queen, in short, cannot recall, as we can who live outside the aphasic linguistic universe of *Tom Thumb*, that her scales are metaphorical and, as such, can operate in the world at large only as a species of verbal shorthand, not as solid things that can be touched or seen. Similarly, the king, by assuming that the well-worn comparison between eyes and windows is fact not figure, can effortlessly transmute whatever covers those eyes into "Window-Blinds" (the pun here is a bonus) and can fool himself into believing that he has witnessed their lifting from the "two open Windows" of Huncamunca's eyes when he announces to her that she can marry Tom Thumb (p. 32). The sign is thus often mistaken for its referent in a language whose words and ideas have gone their separate ways.

Although this brief catalogue does not begin to exhaust the "excellences" of *Tom Thumb*, it does nevertheless set forth the major

68

characteristics of the play's "Supernatural" style in several of its most prominent manifestations. Since the other stylistic features of the work merely ring changes on the patterns of disjunction between words and ideas we have already examined, they need not detain us at this point. The misuse of language is so central to the structure of *Tom Thumb* that it even accounts for the presence of an episode which seems to undermine the unity of the play, as J.T. Hillhouse remarks in one of his notes, and which Fielding omitted from *The Tragedy of Tragedies*, an indication, perhaps, that he too may have arrived at that conclusion as he revised and expanded his original script.[23]

The episode in question depicts the learned debate between two physicians who attempt to diagnose the cause of Tom Thumb's unexpected death by engaging in the usual equivocations of their profession. To conceal the meaninglessness of their evasive quibbling, they embellish their speeches with polysyllables of dubious etymological provenance like *"Diaphormane"* and *"Peripilusis"* and with references to ancient medical authorities whose works they have obviously not read very closely, if at all (p. 34). What little credibility they salvage after their circuitous mumblings is shattered by the news that Tom Thumb is still alive and that their dead patient was actually a monkey dressed in the little hero's "Habit" (p. 35), a sad commentary both on their professional acumen and on the protagonist's pretensions to tragic stature.

Although these two mock doctors belong more properly in the comic world of Molière and consequently do not fit very snugly into the heroic mold of Fielding's "Grubstreet" tragedy, they appear in *Tom Thumb* because their mystifying argot reflects the play's central concern with the "Abuse of Speech," not to mention that these scenes would have been hilarious in performance, as the two actors impersonating these quacks would have no doubt shaken their heads in mock solemnity, tugged at their chins, and scratched their empty pates while speaking their ludicrous lines. Still, Fielding chose to delete these sure-fire scenes from *The Tragedy of Tragedies*, not so much, I would suggest, because he realized that a series of scenes mocking physicians has little place in a parody of heroic tragedy as because the type of linguistic abuse represented in this medical interlude differs significantly from that found in the rest of the play. Unlike other characters in *Tom Thumb*, the two physicians misuse language deliberately, to mask their ignorance and deceive others; they manipulate language while those around them are victims of it. Whereas the hapless king and his subjects are unwitting participants in the play's linguistic corruption because of the inherent defectiveness of their "Supernatural" language, the two physicians generate their own brand of chaos out of a language they can control well enough to achieve their dishonest rhetorical purposes. The former are sincere in their linguistic stupidity and vacuity; the latter are hypocrites who distort language for their own selfish ends.

The satiric target of the physicians' episode in *Tom Thumb*, then, is not so much the abuse of language per se as the conscious abuse of language and learning for the sake of obfuscation and duplicity. And since the abuse of learning is the principal target of the critical apparatus of *The Tragedy of Tragedies*, this episode became redundant when Fielding decided to make its satiric impulses the dominant force of the published version of his revised play. He did not need, in other words, to poke fun locally at what he intended to satirize more comprehensively in his preface and notes. In this respect the same episode that violated the satiric coherence of his acting play might well have provided Fielding with the germ for the scriblerian machinery of his reading play. It is only a short distance from the learned nonsense of the two court physicians to the profound lucubrations of H. Scriblerus Secundus.[24]

When *The Tragedy of Tragedies* opened on 24 March 1731, with *The Letter Writers* as its afterpiece, it was considerably longer and more complex than *Tom Thumb*, though the essential plot and linguistic "excellences" of the original remained basically unaltered. Fielding had expanded the brief scenes of his popular afterpiece into an evening's main entertainment of three acts by adding several characters and complicating the relationships among them. By multiplying his romantic triangles, he heightened and made more ridiculous his characters' conflict between love and honor—one of the central themes of heroic tragedy, which he had explored only superficially in his first version—while providing more plausible motivations for their actions, though he retained, with one crucial change, the wonderfully unmotivated carnage of his final scene.

70

For instance, Grizzle, without a love interest in the earlier play, now vies with Tom Thumb for the affections of Huncamunca, so that his jealousy no longer stems from mere court intrigue but from a more noble cause. The king, equally free of amorous entanglements in the first version, falls prey to the abundant charms of Glumdalca in the sequel while she, in turn, pines for Tom Thumb and thus becomes the rival of the queen and Huncamunca. The practical Huncamunca, however, solves her conflicts between love and honor and between lovers by deciding to marry both Tom Thumb and Grizzle. As she tells the latter,

> My ample Heart for more than one has Room,
> A Maid like me, Heaven form'd at least for two,
> I married him, and now I'll marry you.[25]

Unfortunately, her humble attempt to copy the "happy State of Giantism" (p. 56), for which the queen so envies the twenty-times-married Glumdalca, backfires, and she ends up looking forward to her wedding night without the comforting presence of either of her two husbands, a bleak prospect she renders in a ponderous simile whose bathetic triteness serves to emphasize the true worth of such heroic conflicts in "modern Tragedy":

> I, who this Morn, of two chose which to wed,
> May go again this Night alone to Bed;
> So have I seen some wild unsettled Fool,
> Who had her Choice of this, and that Joint Stool;
> To give the Preference to either, loath
> And fondly coveting to sit on both:
> While the two Stools her Sitting Part confound,
> Between 'em both fall Squat upon the Ground.[26]

In addition to these bizarre romantic complications, Fielding gave his Haymarket audiences ocular proof of Tom Thumb's "might" by showing them the giantess Glumdalca even though, like Swift's Glumdalclitch, she is somewhat less than gigantic, "by a Foot, / Shorter than all her Subject Giants" (p. 56). He also depicted the little hero's slaying of the rebellious Grizzle, a substantial improvement for a character whose only deed of "might" in the original *Tom Thumb* had been the killing of the bailiff and his follower. To enhance further his protagonist's heroic stature, Fielding inserted into his new script a "Prophetick Part" (p. 92), as Scriblerus calls it, modeled after the prophecies of *imperium* in Homer's *Odyssey*, Vergil's *Aeneid*, and particularly the third book of Pope's *Dunciad* (1728; 1729). In this truly "Supernatural" scene, which also strengthens the structure of the work, Merlin foretells Tom Thumb's "fatal End" (p. 92), so that when that end comes, neither the hero nor the spectators are taken by surprise, as they undoubtedly were in the earlier play. Merlin thus makes specific the vague omens of Tom Thumb's "Grandmamma" (p. 65; cf. *Tom Thumb*, p. 30), while lending a certain measure of dignity to them. He also consoles the hero for his woeful destiny by prophesying that his life will become the subject of the play we are now watching:

> See from a far a Theatre arise;
> There, Ages yet unborn, shall Tribute pay
> To the Heroick Actions of this Day:
> Then Buskin Tragedy at length shall choose
> Thy Name the best Supporter of her Muse.
> (p. 92)

Fielding reserved the most significant departure from his original plan, however, for the closing scenes of his new play, in which he substituted the ghost of Gaffar Thumb for that of his illustrious son. This change eliminated the improbable second killing of Tom Thumb which, though the most memorable episode from the first play, had almost immediately become the object of derision of those who claimed that Fielding's piece had "been intended," in Scriblerus's words, as "a Burlesque on the loftiest Parts of Tragedy, and designed to banish what we generally call Fine Things, from the Stage." [27]

That Fielding dropped this theatrically effective scene from *The Tragedy of Tragedies*, after hastening to defend himself from its "Kriticks" in the preface to *Tom Thumb*, suggests that he acknowledged, at least in part, the truth of the charge. He may have sincerely intended his "Burlesque" as an attack on bad heroic tragedy, but the facts seemed to speak otherwise. London had flocked to see *Tom Thumb* not because the play was recognized as a serious call for theatrical reform but because it was all jolly good fun, "a tragedy that," as Rakel says in *The Letter Writers*, "makes me laugh." [28] Fielding had, in a sense, taken the easy way out by turning heroic tragedy into a cheap money-making species of entertainment; he had not bothered to offer a serious alternative. Those with vested interests were quick to point out how the young dramatist was profiting from catering to the town's depraved taste while professing that he meant to reform. So long as *Tom Thumb* and similarly mindless productions held the stage, they argued, legitimate drama did not stand a chance. Fielding had already taken steps to exonerate himself from this charge of artistic frivolity and opportunism by attempting a serious play that would demonstrate that his indulgence in these "unshaped monsters of a wanton brain" was simply a way of keeping body and soul together while he assayed finer things.[29] *The Modern Husband*, however, would circulate in manuscript for a year and would not reach the boards until the following season. In the meantime, *The Tragedy of Tragedies* would have to answer his detractors by reiterating the satiric purposes of *Tom Thumb* in a more explicit—though undramatic—fashion.

When *The Tragedy of Tragedies* was published, it offered its readers not only the acting play, but also the learned commentary of its editor and chief admirer, the scholarly H. Scriblerus Secundus. Like Swift's Grub Street hack and "publisher" in *A Tale of a Tub* (1710) or Gulliver in his captious letter to his publisher-cousin in *Gulliver's Travels* (1727), Fielding's Scriblerus argues that previous editions of the work were "imperfect" and "surreptitious" copies and that the text he now presents is the only reliable one. Moreover, he protests that despite the attributions of "some ill-meaning People," he is not the author of the play but only its humble editor, "more capable," as he phrases it, "of doing Justice to our Author, than any other Man, as I have given my self more Pains to arrive at a thorough Understanding of this little Piece, having for ten Years together read nothing else; in which time, I think I may modestly presume, with the help of my English Dictionary, to comprehend all the Meanings of every Word of it" (p. 42). Like any other devoted scholar, Scriblerus is more than happy to share the fruits of his "Endeavours" with his readers in his preface and notes.

As a result of this decade of close analysis, Scriblerus can now disclose that the play under scrutiny is the Elizabethan original of all contemporary heroic tragedies, *the* tragedy of tragedies,[30] the work perhaps of "Shakespear" himself, though, like the cautious

73

scholar he is, he hesitates to push his point too far and advances it only as a suggestion.[31] If Don Tragedio can boast that he owes nothing to previous heroic tragedians, Scriblerus, in his quiet and reasonable way, can do even better: he can document that *The Tragedy of Tragedies* is not indebted to the English heroic tradition because it is the matrix of that tradition. With Scriblerus's editorial help and specious deductions, *The Tragedy of Tragedies* manages to validate, by exemplifying how "the People of our Age shall be Ancestors," that seemingly alogical Cibberian sentence cited in the preface to *Tom Thumb*. This uncanny ability to pervert time, space, and language is, as we have seen, one of the supreme "excellences" of "modern Tragedy," a genre with no memory, no past, and no future. In Scriblerus it finds, at last, a critic perfectly attuned to its peculiarities.

Having established the date of the play, Scriblerus then proceeds "to a regular Examination of the Tragedy" by treating "separately of the Fable, the Moral, the Characters, the Sentiments, and the Diction" (p. 43), a solemn disquisition, full of misinterpretations and mistranslations of classical sources, that takes up the rest of his preface. Evidence for his claim that "this little Piece" is the garden from which all modern tragedians have culled their poetic "Flowers" appears in his footnotes,[32] in which he also corrects the misreadings of previous critics of the play, the most notorious of whom is a "carping" fault-finder reminiscent of Dennis, whose political and aesthetic prejudices are parodied within the play itself in Grizzle's "for Liberty we fight, / And Liberty the Mustard is of Life," a passage which elicits, in turn, a note that dismisses the objections of "Dennis" by quoting a line from Dennis's *Liberty Asserted* (1704).[33] The views of Bentley, Burmann, Scaliger, Wotton, and several other scholars and would-be scholars also come under the sharp eye of the indefatigable annotator. All in all, the published version of *The Tragedy of Tragedies* treated its readers to a mock scholarly feast of a scope and wit surpassed in previous eighteenth-century English literature only by *A Tale of a Tub* and *The Dunciad Variorum* (1729), the last of which provided Fielding with the structure of his commentary on a text-within as well as the inspiration for his obtuse yet sometimes strangely illuminating Scriblerus. Fielding hoped that his scriblerian preface and notes would silence

74

his attackers once and for all, not only by underlining his allegiance to his scriblerian predecessors, but also by showing that those very absurdities the "Kriticks" so gleefully singled out in his "little Piece" were duplicated in at least forty-two plays they had once applauded vigorously and still continued to enjoy in revivals,[34] that what they regarded as "Fine Things" were nothing more than the hackneyed conventions of an exhausted genre.

The scriblerian machinery of *The Tragedy of Tragedies*, however, could be enjoyed only by its readers. If Fielding's most significant innovation in *Tom Thumb* had been the elimination of the rehearsal structure of *The Author's Farce*, in the reading version of the play he had sought a substitute for it by writing a preface detailing his satiric intentions. This effort to explain, to avoid being misunderstood, culminates in the critical scaffolding of *The Tragedy of Tragedies*. Here H. Scriblerus Secundus, by directing the reader's attention to the satiric object, performs a function similar to that of Luckless in *The Author's Farce*. But Scriblerus is clearly not so bright or perceptive as Luckless, so that he resembles more Buckingham's Bayes, the brainless bard who, by pointing his finger at the "excellences" of his play, unwittingly reveals his most absurd lapses in taste and dramatic presentation. The difference is, of course, that while Bayes and Luckless discover the infelicities in their own plays and thereby allude to the bathetic features of the works their plays are supposed to parody, Scriblerus cites the actual passages from Banks, Dryden, Lee, Rowe, and other heroic playwrights which *The Tragedy of Tragedies* is intended to satirize. The scriblerian machinery of *The Tragedy of Tragedies* is, in short, the reading equivalent of the acting rehearsal form, though by exploiting the more expansive medium of the written page, it allowed Fielding to be more direct and specific in his explosion of what his contemporaries considered "the loftiest Parts of Tragedy."

Fielding may not have been entirely comfortable with the risks he was taking in the acting *Tom Thumb* and *The Tragedy of Tragedies* and therefore felt compelled to include these additional satiric pointers in the published products,[35] but the plays in themselves, in performance, nonetheless marked a crucial stage in his understanding of dramatic possibilities. He now knew that he could write a satiric irregular play without an author-within, that he could let the satiric object satirize itself. Obviously, by choosing to ridicule the already ludicrous effusions of "modern Tragedy," he had picked an easy target. But the idea had worked. And though he would continue to have his doubts about his new satiric method and would seldom dispense with the author-within in his subsequent irregular plays, he would not forget the lessons he had learned in *Tom Thumb* and would manipulate those future authors-within to achieve dramatic effects unsuspected either by Buckingham or indeed by his own younger self in *The Author's Farce*. At the same time, he also confirmed what he had already known in *The Author's Farce*: scriblerian satire works best—or, more accurately, is less likely to be misinterpreted—when Scriblerus is present to underscore it. In the three versions of *The Grub-Street Opera*, Scriblerus would finally leave the comfort of his writing table and appear on stage to introduce and comment on his dramatic offspring, as Fielding would incorporate the reading matter of *Tom Thumb* and *The Tragedy of Tragedies* into the several acting scripts of what proved to be the last of his scriblerian plays. But before lowering the curtain on the last scene of H. Scriblerus Secundus's dramatic career, we shall return to the Little Theatre for a brief interlude. It is Midsummer Eve and Fielding's "heroic Muse" is about to sing.

CHAPTER 4

The Generous Method of
the Heroic Muse:
Rape upon Rape

THE 1730 theater season, as we have seen, was a rewarding one for Fielding, both financially and artistically. *The Temple Beau* returned him to the London stage after an absence of two years; *The Author's Farce* and *Tom Thumb* established him as the most exciting playwright in England since Gay. As the season waned, Fielding put on his fourth play of the year, *Rape upon Rape; or, The Justice Caught in His Own Trap*. This five-act comedy opened on 23 June at the Little Theatre, ran for eight nights, and, with revisions and a new title *(The Coffee-House Politician)*, it was revived in the autumn at Lincoln's Inn Fields.[1] Unlike *The Author's Farce* and *Tom Thumb*, it was regular in structure, a reading play featuring the antics of Politic, a quixotic character who reads, rereads, and misreads newspapers and forgets, as Justice Worthy exclaims in disbelief, "the loss of his only daughter!"[2] But this "political humour"—Worthy's words again—is not Fielding's primary focus, though the play, as several critics have argued, has political implications, with its original title explicitly alluding to the most notorious rape case of the day—Dabble remembers "to have seen in some newspaper a story not very different from this" (5.4[145])—the trial and conviction of Colonel Francis Charteris, "Rapemaster General of Great Britain" and associate of the prime minister.[3] Fielding's allusive title firmly grounds his play in contemporary events while the play itself, by juxtaposing the legal philosophies of Justice Squeezum and Justice Worthy, explores the deficiencies of a judicial system that

77

would let a convicted rapist go free. This concern with specific social issues marks a radical departure from the general satire of *The Temple Beau* and a step toward the harsh moral comedy of *The Modern Husband*, a play Fielding had begun to work on at about this time.

The prologue announces Fielding's intention to particularize his satirical attacks. The author begins by giving his audience a brief history of the origin and decline of true satire:

> In ancient Greece, the infant Muse's school,
> Where vice first felt the pen of ridicule,
> With honest freedom and impartial blows
> The Muse attacked each vice as it arose:
> No grandeur could the mighty villain screen
> From the just satire of the comic scene:
> No titles could the daring poet cool,
> Nor save the great right honourable fool.
> They spared not even the aggressor's name,
> And public villainy felt public shame.

This "generous method," however, has "been disused" because "power" now protects the vicious: "While beaus, and cits, and squires, our scenes afford, / Justice preserves the rogues who wield her sword." Fielding's "heroic Muse" will attempt a return to the "honest freedom" of ancient Greece: "Vice, clothed with power, she combats with her pen, / And, fearless, dares the lion in his den." But, as the allusion to Daniel suggests, Fielding's Muse is also Christian; while unsparing of "the conscious knave," she will make smile "the uncorrupt and good" man who finds "no mark for satire in his generous mind." Unlike the "comic muse" of *The Temple Beau,* the "heroic Muse" does not merely "scoff at vice, and laugh its crimes away"; her "generous method" requires the active cooperation of the good men and women in the playhouse. Their sober, benevolent smiles should not be confused with the Hobbesian, selfish laughter aroused by other muses. The "heroic Muse"does not simply expose the wicked to ridicule; she urges the virtuous not only to "smile" at the actions of the vicious but also to act to eradicate those evils. Generosity, for Fielding, requires compassion as well as reforming action; it entails social involvement and the abil-

78

ity to pass impartial judgment on the deeds and misdeeds of our fellow human beings.

As we shall see, the play itself does not appear to follow this "generous method" of particular satire. There is, in other words, no character the audience can identify specifically with Colonel Charteris. But, as Bertrand Goldgar has observed, Fielding did not need to expose Colonel Charteris upon the stage by name: "given [the] atmosphere in the spring of 1730 . . . there can be little doubt that audiences at the Haymarket . . . would have immediately connected [the play] with the Charteris affair."[4] The satiric object, in short, need not appear on stage because Fielding can rely on the "generous minds" of his patrons to make the right connections. And once those connections have been made, they inform the audience's response to the action unfolding on stage. Then, as the topical connections recede into the background, the phrase "rape upon rape" begins to function as a metaphor for the abuses of power of Walpole and his minions, while the dramatic confrontation between the perverse Justice Squeezum and the admirable Justice Worthy becomes an emblem of the struggle in English society between the abettors of corruption and the preservers of traditional values.

Fielding's invocation of the "heroic Muse" thus suggests that his conception of regular comedy is changing because his conception of the relationship between the playwright and his audience is also changing. After writing two irregular, acting plays—plays that emphasize and illustrate the necessary cooperation between the dramatist and his public—Fielding begins to see the five-act comedy, long the playground of ludicrous beaus, cits, and squires, as a potential medium for serious discussion of social issues. And Fielding introduces this new element into regular comedy by returning to older dramatic forms, by following the example of the Greeks, particularly of Aristophanes, a man who, in Fielding's words, "exerted [his] Genius in the Service of his Country. He attack'd and expos'd its Enemies and Betrayers with a Boldness and Integrity, which must endear his Memory to every True and Sincere Patriot."[5] Like Shaw at the end of the nineteenth century, Fielding begins to transform the subject matter of the well-made

79

play because, like Shaw, he has grasped that the playhouse, if the playwright so legislates, can become once more a public forum for political and social dialogue, a powerful instrument of moral reformation.

Fielding's reformation of regular comedy does not occur all at once; as always, he introduces the new while preserving what he can of the old. *Rape upon Rape* exhibits many features of regular comedy (a love plot, humorous characters like Politic and Sotmore, mistaken identities and discoveries, and the like), but these features are arranged differently. Instead of using love and marriage as the unifying themes of his plot, Fielding constructs his play around the concept of law. The last words of the play are spoken not by one of the reunited lovers, as they are in both *Love in Several Masques* and *The Temple Beau*, but by Justice Worthy. He passes judgment on the actions of Justice Squeezum and pronounces sentence, having observed, before this final judgment, that Sotmore's excessive fondness for the bottle is a "beastly pleasure," not the "humour" of an honest man, as Ramble would have it (5.6 [156]). These sober moral observations are softened somewhat by the ribald epilogue, spoken by the actress playing Hilaret, though her closing wish— that the "beauteous kind spectators of tonight" may "never know that dreadful thing, a Rape"—can be realized only in a society where vice is punished and excessive behavior moderated.

The play opens with a disruption of order. Hilaret is making preparations to leave her father's house and elope with Constant. She is "horribly frighted at the thoughts of throwing myself into the power of a young fellow" (1.1 [79]), but she is reassured by her worldly-wise maid Cloris that there is little to fear. Still, Hilaret has reservations about her "lover's sincerity," though she is so governed by her "passion" that she cannot help herself. Politic interrupts the confabulations of his daughter and her maid. In the ensuing exchange the audience discovers that Hilaret is not the only character ruled by passion. An avid reader of newspapers, Politic interprets his conflict with his daughter in terms of their reading habits: they cannot agree because she reads romances. She, in turn, believes that Politic has neglected his paternal duties because of his political obsession. The clash between private and public concerns indicates that there is a dangerous imbalance in this society. Politic's dual sacrifice of his daughter's interest and of his career as merchant in favor of his risible projects and misdirected preoccupation with state affairs finds a parallel in the judicial perversions of Justice Squeezum, a man who uses his public office to gratify his private vices. If for Mandeville society could work properly only by turning private vices into public benefits, for Fielding the job was to eliminate both private and public vices by making sure that private virtue would coincide with and promote the common good.[6] Given the existence and the machinations of evil men and women, the proper ordering of society can be achieved only by legal means. It is crucial, therefore, that the law be enforced by the best men in the commonwealth.

Justice Worthy is, of course, one of these unimpeachable men, a modern embodiment of the philosopher-king of Plato's *Republic*, but he does not triumph until the end. In this respect the second act mirrors the movement of the play. It begins with the introduction of Squeezum and concludes with the moral precepts of Worthy. In between, Squeezum's machinations are allowed to display themselves fully. The act opens with an allusion to the beginning of *The Beggar's Opera*. In Gay's opening scene, Peachum and Filch are discussing the disposal of their customers, some of whom must hang or be transported, while those who are still useful can continue to ply their trade. A receiver of stolen goods, Peachum keeps his thieves in line by handing them over to Lockit, the corrupt jailer, when they fail to come up with the appropriate loot. For his part, Lockit allows Peachum to operate safely so long as the bribes remain frequent and plentiful. By combining the offices of Peachum and Lockit, and holding, moreover, a place on the bench, Squeezum is a much more powerful menace to society than Gay's rogues. Peachum and Lockit can—in the words of the play's first song—only "be-rogue one another" and those within their immediate sphere of influence in the London underworld. Squeezum, on the other hand, as *Rape upon Rape* dramatizes, can peach and squeeze everybody. While Gay's beggar wishes to show the analogies between low life and high, Fielding aims to underscore the interpenetration of evil, its all-pervasive influence on every member of society.

Squeezum's discussion with Quill begins with a reference to

81

the justice's "protection" of bawdy houses—a most fitting topic, given the play's title and Walpole's apparent protection of Charteris. Unfortunately for Squeezum, Mother Bilkum refuses to be bilked any longer; she believes that she can bypass her old protector and bribe a jury herself. For his part, Squeezum is certain that he can continue to "regulate the juries": that is, he can stack them with knaves in his debt. Squeezum's view of justice is captured not only in his rape of language—he redefines *protection* and *regulate* to suit his evil purposes—but also in his use of metaphors and similes, another kind of linguistic duplicity: "The laws are turnpikes, only made to stop people who walk on foot, and not to interrupt those who drive through them in their coaches.—The laws are like a game at loo, where a blaze of court cards is always secure, and the knaves are the safest cards in the pack" (2.2 [94]). For Squeezum, the laws do not constitute a single, absolute system, contained and meaningful in itself. In fact, they might not even exist, since he can speak of them in figures and define them in terms of his own mercenary system of values. Squeezum's language is not denotative but connotative: it is a game in which the speaker who can legislate the signification of words has the winning hand.

Men like Squeezum recognize that societal structures are gamelike: the trick is to know the rules, not to abide by them like honest men and women, but to control them, to twist them to serve selfish ends. These wicked men and women, however, fail to see that life in society, while apparently gamelike, is also in earnest, that human actions have moral consequences, that, at the end of the game, the original rules will prevail and the good will hold the "court cards." Paradoxically, this perfectly regulated society seldom exists in reality; it can only be written about in books or depicted on stage, in plays like *Rape upon Rape*, as an ideal to be emulated. In this respect, the "generous method" of the "heroic Muse" gives us a truer image of what we ought to be like than life does because the game is regulated by the ideal legislator, the good dramatist. In life, men like Squeezum and Charteris usually win; in the theater, they are exposed and drummed out of society. In life, these masters of what Fielding calls the "art of thriving" control the performance; in the playhouse, they must submit to the judgment of a higher dramatic court.

Rape upon Rape

The theater as courtroom is indeed the controlling image of *Rape upon Rape*. As we have seen, the concept of judgment also informs Fielding's other plays. In *Love in Several Masques* and *The Temple Beau*, men and women are taught to read themselves and each other correctly, to peruse for inner meaning, not to skim the surface. In *The Author's Farce* and *Tom Thumb*, the link between reading and judgment is expanded to include another, often mindless, activity—play-watching. In *Rape upon Rape* the connection between the theater and the courtroom is explicitly enacted. The audience, acting as jurors, are privileged to go behind the scenes, to observe Squeezum's performance without benefit of his screen of legal respectability. The playwright, in his role as attorney for the prosecution, offers his audience incontrovertible evidence of Squeezum's villainy, evidence that is gradually presented to the other dramatis personae and fully revealed only in the "trial" (Isabella's word) at the end. Then, the dramatist, by letting the unworthy justice think that he is the author of his own play, that he controls all his plots, leads him into his own trap. Squeezum himself points out the analogy between legal and dramatic matters to Worthy and the audience: "Truly, brother Worthy, I think the makers of laws, and the executors of them, should be free of them; as authors and actors are free of the playhouse" (5.6 [147]). As we have seen and shall continue to see, Fielding's plays are full of would-be playwrights whose plots fail, not because they are ignorant of the nexus between world and stage, of the histrionic basis of human action, but because they are so caught up in their own performances as dramatists that they forget about the possibility that they might be actors in a larger play. Squeezum's plots fail because he has usurped offices that do not belong to him. Like Wilding in *The Temple Beau* and Modern in *The Modern Husband*, he reveals that he is an inept maker and executor; he cannot complete his play successfully, and a final act, in which he is unmasked as a hypocrite, as a mere actor, must be supplied by other hands. Worthy triumphs because he performs his proper role in society; in acting well his part as executor of the laws of England, he follows the script written by an authority higher than himself.

Squeezum, however, is not the only plotter in *Rape upon Rape*. The action of the play consists, in fact, of the clash of several plots,

83

all of which fail. Hilaret's plot to elope with Constant, which generates the plot of *Rape upon Rape*, misfires badly. She finds herself in the clutches of Ramble's lascivious plot, a plot she tries to undermine by promising to meet him at a "corner tavern" (1.9 [90]). Ramble, an old practitioner of the art of walking the streets, does not fall for this ploy; in the ensuing scuffle, Hilaret cries "rape" and they are both taken to Squeezum. Meanwhile, Constant attempts to rescue a damsel in distress and is arrested for rape; like Ramble, he is a "knight-errant," though their quixotic quests take different forms. Politic's plots, played out on that "map of the whole world" that is his head (1.5 [84]), may be imaginary, but they have contributed to his daughter's "mad frolic" (1.1 [79]). Squeezum himself has another plot concealed under his legal robe, though this one is not acted out in *Rape upon Rape*, principally because Fielding was already devoting a whole play to this subject. Suspicious that his wife is plotting against him—as indeed she is, and it is her evidence that convicts him at the end—Squeezum wishes to "discover" her in adultery and thereby take advantage of the "very wholesome laws against cuckoldom" (4.1 [125]).

The central action of *Rape upon Rape* hinges on the "most notable plot" (3.13 [123]), as Constant tells Ramble, "invented" by Hilaret and executed by her and Sotmore—"Mr. Hogshead here is to play his part too" (ibid.), adds Constant—to catch the corrupt justice in his own trap. Unlike plots concocted by lovers in Fielding's other plays—for example, Wisemore's elaborate deception of Lady Matchless in *Love in Several Masques*—this one is thwarted by Squeezum's counterplot. In *Rape upon Rape*, the lovers do not succeed because their plot is unlawful. The law does not allow the individual to make up evidence, even if that evidence is fabricated to convict a "sneaking rascal" (4.7 [133]). In their zeal to expose Squeezum, Hilaret and her friends are perverting the legal system to suit their selfish ends and thus have begun to resemble their tormentor. The right order of society cannot be achieved by letting everyone, even those with the best intentions, be free with the laws. As Worthy observes, England boasts "as wholesome laws as any kingdom upon earth" (p. 146); the problem is that they are being executed by rogues like Squeezum, who adulterate wholesome laws to line their own pockets. Given the evidence of *The*

Modern Husband, it is clear that Fielding believed that at least one law in the books was not very wholesome. But the emphasis in *Rape upon Rape* is on the proper execution of existing laws, an issue that had become the subject of public debate after the pardon of Colonel Charteris.

Fielding's concern with the proper conduct of magistrates might suggest that *Rape upon Rape* is less than entertaining. Although the play contains "some things almost solemn enough for a Sermon"[7]—to borrow Parson Adams's words on *The Conscious Lovers*—it serves up its instruction with a most generous helping of delight. *Rape upon Rape* is an extremely funny play, nowhere more so than in its depiction of Hilaret's "notable plot" to entrap Squeezum. Indeed, its comic treatment of a most serious issue might seem flippant at times. Rape is not a humorous subject, and the potentially offending title was changed by the time the play was revived at Lincoln's Inn Fields. As noted in the beginning, Fielding chose the subject of rape because of its topicality: he then uses the historical event as a point of departure, as a symbol, as a means of addressing the real source of the problem. Thus, the meaning of "rape" is expanded to include all violations of human freedom; to guarantee that freedom, Fielding argues, the laws must be properly enforced. It is no accident, then, that most of the characters in the play end up in prison at one point or another, or that Squeezum's jailhouse provides the setting for most of the action. Even those characters who are not literally imprisoned are prisoners of their unruly passions. And Ramble, for most of the play, believes that his Isabella has drowned, until in the closing scene, she, like Shakespeare's Marina, is "refunded" from the sea. *Rape upon Rape*, in short, stresses the idea of confinement, physical or mental, and suggests how English citizens might be rescued from their confinement. As Worthy puts it, "I long to see the time when here, as in Holland, the traveller may walk unmolested, and carry his riches openly with him" (5.5 [146]).

Still, even after this explanation of Fielding's purpose and procedures, more needs to be said about his "generous method" in *Rape upon Rape* to understand why he might have found it less than satisfactory. The key word here, as throughout the play, is *generous*. By letting several of his characters redefine this adjective to fit their ends—Sotmore speaks of the "generous liquor," Mrs. Squeezum of her "generous pity"—Fielding indicates the dangers of the concept of generosity. It can be adapted, twisted, rendered meaningless. One way to render the word meaningless is by being too generous, too forgiving. This type of generosity screens the culprit, spares him from the justice he deserves. In this sense the playwright himself might be guilty: he is perhaps too generous, too charitable, in his depiction of evil. Justice Squeezum may be a villain, but he is also a buffoon. When he first appears, he seems threatening enough, but that threat is reduced almost immediately by the revelation that this scheming justice is suffering under the yoke of matrimonial tyranny. And when he woos Hilaret at the tavern, in a scene that recalls the uproarious assignation between Aquilina and Antonio in *Venice Preserv'd* (3.1), he reaches the sublime of the ridiculous: "Give me a kiss for that.—Thou shalt find me a young lover, a vigorous young lover too.—Hit me a slap in the face, do—Bow-wow! Bow-wow! I'll eat up your clothes.—Come, what will you drink? White or red? Women love white best.—Boy, bring half a pint of mountain.—Come, sit down; do, sit down.—Come, now let us hear the story how you were first debauched.—Come—that I may put it down in my history at home. I have the history of all the women's ruin that ever I lay with, and I call it, THE HISTORY OF MY OWN TIMES" (4.6 [129–30]).[8]

After this farcical performance, it is difficult to take Justice Squeezum seriously. He is a laughable old lecher, described by Sotmore as "an old withered maypole . . . with these spindle shanks, that weezle face, that crane's neck of a body" (4.7 [132]).[9] Although Squeezum's stratagems almost triumph at the end, he does not arouse fear but guffaws. Like Wilding, he boasts of sexual conquests—"I have done execution in my time," he tells Hilaret (p. 130)—for which there is no evidence; his history, one suspects, ought to occupy a prominent place on Politic's reading list, perhaps next to the latest issue of the *Lying Post*. As Worthy exclaims, in his only funny line in the play, when Squeezum cries that "a vile woman hath conspired to swear a rape against me": "A rape against you! foolish jade! Why, your very face would acquit you" (5.6 [146–47]). In short, while the "heroic Muse" might inspire the playwright to specify who the culprits are, her "generous method" perhaps muffles the impact of the hit. *The Modern Husband,* as we shall see, would change all that: fidelity to nature and to truth requires not generosity but a method closer to Swift's *saeva indignatio.* We now turn to Fielding's tribute to another one of his scriblerian models as the young dramatist set out to moralize the song of *The Beggar's Opera* and thus reform the genre invented by Gay.

CHAPTER 5

A Master Honored
and Improved:
The Grub-Street Opera and
The Beggar's Opera

O F THE THREE acting scripts of Scriblerus Secundus's ballad opera, only one was ever staged before a Haymarket audience. *The Welsh Opera* replaced the uninspired *Letter Writers* as the afterpiece to *The Tragedy of Tragedies* on 22 April 1731, and appeared nine more times that summer, five of them with the politically explosive adaptation of *The Fall of Mortimer*, before Fielding, always eager to please the public and turn a larger profit, decided to interrupt the run and transform his popular afterpiece "into a whole Night's Entertainment, intituled, The Grub-street Opera" which, as the advertisement in *The Daily Post* (5 June 1731) assured its readers, was "now in Rehearsal."[1] The sequel is well known.[2] Owing to government intervention, either in the form of outright suppression or, as Bertrand Goldgar more plausibly suggests, in the more discreet guise of a bribe to ensure the young dramatist's silence, *The Grub-Street Opera* was never performed and has remained, except for those few rehearsals in June 1731, Fielding's only true reading play.[3]

When it became clear that *The Grub-Street Opera* would never be acted, E. Rayner published *The Welsh Opera*, apparently without the author's knowledge and cooperation. Rayner was also responsible, it now appears, for the publication, in early August 1731, of *The Genuine Grub-Street Opera*.[4] This second acting script of the play

88

was purportedly "Printed and Sold," in the words of its title page, "for the Benefit of the Comedians of the NEW THEATRE in the *Haymarket*."[5] Although the players protested their innocence, it is obvious that somebody from within the playhouse had provided Rayner with a prompter's copy on both occasions and that Fielding, unable to control the circumstances of publication of his work, had ample cause to vent his anger and frustration at "the intolerable and scandalous Nonsense of this notorious Paper Pyrate," especially when a good portion of that "scandalous Nonsense" had political implications and might well undermine his future bids for Walpole's patronage.[6]

The first two acting versions of *The Grub-Street Opera*, then, were published in 1731, both without Fielding's approval and supervision, both "incorrect and spurious" copies full of printer's errors and other more serious mistakes. As a result of Rayner's paper piracy, the critic of the play can accept only the final script, *The Grub-Street Opera*, as the genuine text because it alone was issued with Fielding's consent and presumably embodies the work as he intended it to be. The fact that the piece, in spite of the 1731 date on its title page, may have been printed as late as June 1755, by Andrew Millar, further reinforces its textual authority.[7] As Fielding's friend and publisher, Millar can be trusted to have followed the wishes of his recently deceased client regarding his twice-pilfered play and to have printed an accurate and reliable text. Finally, it must be admitted that neither *The Welsh Opera* nor *The Genuine Grub-Street Opera* is as artistically interesting or as dramatically coherent as *The Grub-Street Opera*. For these reasons, I have chosen the last of Scriblerus Secundus's three acting scripts as my principal reading text.

The Grub-Street Opera is important to the student of Fielding's dramatic career for several reasons. To begin with, it is his first overtly political play as well as his first full-fledged ballad opera. It also pursues the study of the modern "Abuse of Speech" he had begun in *The Author's Farce* and continued in *Tom Thumb* and *The Tragedy of Tragedies;* more significantly, it serves as the testing ground for many of the ideas he was then exploring in a more serious vein in *The Modern Husband*, a work still in progress. It is, finally, the play in which Fielding paid his most handsome homage, through imitation and parody, to the scriblerian author of *The Beggar's Opera*.

From the beginning of his dramatic career Fielding, as we have seen, had to live in the long shadow cast by his scriblerian contemporary. *Love in Several Masques* had an abbreviated tenure of four nights principally because the town had gone wild over Gay's Newgate pastoral. *The Beggar's Opera* ran for sixty-two evenings that first glorious season and continued its unprecedented success the following year by logging well over forty performances, some of them by a children's company known as the Lilliputians, an indication of Rich's willingness to heap novelty on novelty so long as the public paid for it.[8] Under the circumstances, Fielding had been wise to remove himself to Leyden for a while.

Fielding had made his debut on the London theatrical scene at a most unpropitious time for a new playwright, especially for a playwright with his talents and sensibilities. Not only was his regular comedy an inadequate alternative to Gay's unconventional ballad opera, but he soon discovered many affinities between his artistic temperament and that of his more famous colleague. Fielding must have asked himself several times during his Dutch sojourn whether the town could and would support another Gay. He must have answered himself in the affirmative because, rather than giving up or fighting his adversary with conventional weapons, he decided to join him, to pay him the compliment of turning him into one of his models. Luckily for Fielding, *The Beggar's Opera* was Gay's last popular work. Both *Polly* (1729), suppressed by Walpole, though an instant cause célèbre and best-seller by subscription, and *Achilles*, a humorless and ponderous affair acted posthumously at Covent Garden in 1733, failed to stir the imagination of the theatrical public, though the latter, thanks to the efforts of the dramatist's friends, held the boards for twenty nights. The master had had his day and would die in 1732. It was time for his pupil to acknowledge his debts to his teacher.

In the several versions of *The Grub-Street Opera* Fielding set out to make more explicit his indebtedness to the third member of the scriblerian triumvirate he had chosen to emulate. If the Scriblerus Secundus of *The Author's Farce* and the *Tom Thumb* plays had been modeled on Pope's Martinus Scriblerus in particular and more generally on Swift's half-witted authorial personae, the Scriblerus Secundus of *The Grub-Street Opera* was unmistakably the close relation of Gay's dramaturgical beggar. Not that Gay's presence had been totally absent from Fielding's two previous irregular plays. *The Author's Farce*, with its twenty-five songs and its dialogue between Luckless and the player before the puppet show, may be regarded as a direct descendant and parody (see, for example, Air 12) of *The Beggar's Opera*, except that, as Edmond McAdoo Gagey has rightly observed, Fielding's play "may be considered a ballad opera only by courtesy"; its dramatic purposes lie elsewhere, its satiric method points in another direction.[9] In *The What D'ye Call It*, however, as I suggested earlier, Gay may have offered Fielding a model for the farcical rendering of contemporary theatrical entertainments. Gay's definition and justification of his strange dramatic techniques in the preface to his "tragi-comi-pastoral farce" may have furnished his disciple with part of the theoretical basis for his own attack on the pleasures of the town. In addition, the play itself, with its disconcerting disjunction between language and dramatic presentation, might have given the young apprentice the initial idea for the fractured syntax of *Tom Thumb* and *The Tragedy of Tragedies*. But Fielding owed his scriblerian forebear a more pointed tribute. *The Welsh Opera* would begin that tribute; *The Grub-Street Opera* would complete it, honoring the master while improving his work.

Perhaps the most notable feature of the three drafts of *The Grub-Street Opera*—certainly the only feature to receive any extensive critical attention—is their sustained political allegory. Both *The Author's Farce* of 1730 and *Tom Thumb* (in its two versions) contain isolated digs at the ministry, but these scattered allusions never cohere into an antigovernment whole. Occasional references to Tom Thumb as a "great man" or attacks on Cibber's life and works hardly qualify as virulent antiministerial satire, especially when one reads the pages of the *Craftsman* and the *Grub-Street Journal* or scans the scenes of the otherwise insufferably dull and dramatically inept *The Fall of Mortimer*, a piece whose sole purpose was obviously to offend.[10] Fielding scores his political hits in his two earlier plays in passing, to tease and amuse his audience momentarily with a line or word guaranteed to elicit a laugh because of its topical relevance.

The Author's Farce and the *Tom Thumb* plays are literary satires and parodies; they are not political tracts. Finally, as I have argued in my last chapter, the political applications and implications of *Rape upon Rape*, though more explicit, serve primarily as background for the exploration of the larger, more general issue of social order and the crucial role the proper execution of laws plays in maintaining and preserving that order.

The Grub-Street Opera is so glaringly political in nature that we cannot ignore its political message. In this instance, the political critic may be forgiven his zeal. Yet even here we must exercise caution and remember that the document at hand is a play and must be examined as such. One of the problems with an exclusively political analysis of *The Grub-Street Opera* is that once the critic has identified the play's references to Walpole's public and private excesses, to Queen Caroline's well-known influence over her husband, and to Prince Frederick's rumored impotence—to mention only three of the most prominent allusions noted by Cross, Brown, Roberts, and Morrissey—and matched the play's dramatis personae with members of the royal household, the administration, and the Opposition, he has little left to say and usually deems his task of elucidation at an end. A ballad opera of sixty-five songs—in Hume's estimate, "one of the finest ballad operas of its time"[11]—has thus been reduced to the status of political journalism or to what John Loftis has called, if one pardons his anachronism (the work not being published until the next century), "a dramatization of Lord Hervey's *Memoirs*."[12] In short, we still need to deal with the play as a dramatic entity.

I do not, of course, deny the political implications of *The Grub-Street Opera*, which are dramatically important as well as fascinating in their own right; I simply wish to compensate for the present critical imbalance. We shall never understand Fielding's genius as a playwright until we approach his drama in dramatic terms, until we stop combing his plays for evidence of the future novelist or regarding them as chapters in his political autobiography.[13] We must curb the impulse to refer everything in the play to the real world; instead, we must pay attention to the coherent dramatic world which the play represents and explore that world according to its own dramatic rules. That, I would argue, is the first and most

This is real old New Criticism

important context within which all of Fielding's plays must be understood, yet it is precisely this context that is consistently ignored by students of Fielding's dramatic career as they search for other contexts, either in politics or in theater history, while ignoring the plays as plays. Even in *The Historical Register for the Year 1736*, his most political play, Fielding subsumes his political themes under his dramatic design. He was a playwright first, a politician, if he ever thought of himself as one, a distant second. By paying too much attention to individual political allusions, the political critic misses the larger, more significant perspective of the dramatic whole; he needlessly reduces a complex play to a simple-minded political allegory.

That *The Grub-Street Opera* in its several incarnations develops a political theme should come as no surprise to students of eighteenth-century drama. As the most insistently communal of our literary genres, drama, from Aristophanes to George Bernard Shaw, has often provided a public forum for the discussion and exposition of social and political ideas. Politics, never a minor preoccupation of our Restoration and Augustan ancestors, played a prominent role in the tragedies of, among others, Dryden, Otway, Lee, and Rowe. Comedies, for their part, tended to concentrate on social situations, particularly on the vexing question of the proper relations among love, money, and marriage. One of Gay's accomplishments in *The Beggar's Opera* was his fusion of these two contemporary dramatic concerns into one stupendous play. *The Beggar's Opera* managed to combine the satirical with the pathetic, to touch the mind as well as the heart, to satisfy the ear as well as the eye.

The double nature of *The Beggar's Opera* explains, to a very large extent, why the play was so successful. Some liked it for its daring political message, for the sheer pleasure of seeing Walpole and his cohorts gibbeted as rogues. Others delighted in the play's overt appeal—albeit tinged with an irony so fine as to pass virtually undetected—to the softer passions. As James Quin, the actor originally slated to play Macheath, told Richard Cambridge, the audience at the first performance, no doubt puzzled by the novelty of the piece, withheld its applause until roused by Polly's moving plea for her parents' sympathy in Air 12 ("Now Ponder Well, Ye Parents

Dear").[14] Indeed, it is difficult to account for the work's immense popularity in purely political terms, without its music and pageantry, without its love interest, without its parody of the absurdities of Italian opera, without its human and dramatic complexities. Modern critics of *The Beggar's Opera* have been judicious enough to recognize that the political satire, while important, is only part of a larger whole.[15] Critics of *The Grub-Street Opera* have not been so perceptive. It is time to supplement their political findings with an analysis of the neglected features of the play.[16]

The first feature of the play the audience and the reader become aware of is the dramatic intrusion of Scriblerus Secundus. In *The Author's Farce* and the *Tom Thumb* plays Scriblerus, as we have observed, remains offstage, in one as a name on the title page, in the other two as author and editor. While it could be argued that Luckless is a scriblerian figure, the truth is that he is not Scriblerus, that Fielding chose to give his puppet master another name and to use the famous cognomen primarily to associate *The Author's Farce* more closely with the satiric work of Pope, Swift, and Gay. In *Tom Thumb* and *The Tragedy of Tragedies*, however, Scriblerus begins to grow into a character, though only for the reader. With the three versions of *The Grub-Street Opera*, he finally becomes a *theatrical* character; the invisible dramatist and commentator is no longer a series of words on paper, but lives on stage as flesh and blood.

The theatrical fleshing out of Scriblerus Secundus thus creates a dramatic link between the several drafts of *The Grub-Street Opera* and Fielding's earlier scriblerian plays. In this respect it is important to recall that Scriblerus's "new" ballad opera (like Don Tragedio, Scriblerus loves to boast about his novelty) first appeared as the afterpiece to *The Tragedy of Tragedies*. As *The Welsh Opera* opens, Scriblerus alludes to his editorial role in *The Tragedy of Tragedies* by telling the player that he intends "to be a sort of walking notes" to his play. He also discourses on the widespread confusion between tragedy and comedy as well as on the difference between "tragical" and "comical" similes, arguing that the "so have I seen" variety "belongs to tragedy," a fact the audience already knows from listening to the speeches of the ghost and king in the last act of *The Tragedy of Tragedies*.[17] Finally, the second player clinches the connections between main piece and afterpiece by informing Scriblerus that "Mrs. Jones, who played Huncamunca, insists on a dram before she goes on for Madam Apshinken." Incensed by this impertinence, Scriblerus stalks off the stage, promising to "burn my four dozen operas and six dozen of tragedies, and never give 'em another" (p. 78). He will not be a "sort of walking notes" to his play; he will let it make its dramatic point all by itself.

In the Introduction to *The Grub-Street Opera*, however, Fielding omitted all explicit references to *The Tragedy of Tragedies*, no doubt because the revision was meant to be "a whole Night's Entertainment," not the continuation or extension of the earlier play. This point is worth a short digression. Unlike other contemporary playwrights, Fielding wrote his afterpieces to fit the plays they followed on stage, either through specific allusions or through the exploration of similar themes, plots, or other dramatic concerns or devices. Thus in *The Letter Writers* Rakel refers to *The Tragedy of Tragedies*, which the audience has just seen performed, as "a tragedy that makes me laugh"; *Tom Thumb*, as indicated earlier, narrows the focus of the general satire of *The Author's Farce*. An extreme case of this procedure occurs in *Eurydice Hiss'd* (1737) which borrows two of its characters and its rehearsal structure from *The Historical Register*. In this way Fielding creates order out of the usual chaos encouraged by contemporary theatrical practices. In his hands the afterpiece ceased to be a mere afterthought, a way of beefing up an evening's bill of fare, and became an integral part of "a whole Night's Entertainment."

Yet even though *The Grub-Street Opera* was not intended to be the afterpiece to *The Tragedy of Tragedies*, it nonetheless pursues many of the generic and linguistic concerns of the earlier play. The most obvious link between the two plays is, of course, the figure of Scriblerus. The new title of the piece provides another important connection. By calling his revision *The Grub-Street Opera*, Fielding is not primarily attacking the *Grub-Street Journal*, as would appear at first glance. If anything, he is joining the *Journal* in its campaign against Grub Street dunces: he is indicating that Scriblerus's ballad opera is a Grub Street production, concocted by the same type of imagination that dreams up modern tragedies and author's farces. The new title recalls, first of all, the preface to *Tom Thumb*, in which, as we have already observed, Scriblerus enjoins "our (the

95

Grubstreet) Tragical Writers" to choose models more consonant with their abilities. It also alludes to the damning panegyric in the prologue to the same play written, we are informed, "By no Friend of the Author's"—

> Oh glorious Lane!
> O, may thy Authors never write in vain!
> May crowded Theatres ne'er give Applause
> To any other than the *Grub-Street* Cause!

—as well as to Luckless's self-congratulatory and self-mocking speech at the end of *The Author's Farce:*

> Taught by my fate, let never bard despair.
> Though long he drudge and feed on Grub Street air,
> Since him, at last; 'tis possible to see
> As happy and as great a king as me.

In choosing their new title, both Fielding and Scriblerus strengthen the ties between their most recent play and their previous ones. As composed by the denizens of Grub Street, ballad operas are of a piece with puppet shows and "laughing" tragedies.

Scriblerus has written a ballad opera, then, because he is a Grub Street author; the new title merely confirms the obvious. For Fielding, the mindless euphoria with which *The Beggar's Opera* had been received, together with the artistically dubious progeny it had spawned, suggested that Gay's new form had degenerated into another frivolous pleasure of the town, often copied and applauded, but rarely understood. *The Beggar's Opera* had become, in other words, the model for many a Grub Street opera.[18] This is one of the reasons why Fielding incorporates elements of ballad opera into Luckless's puppet show, itself another debased form, though a potentially redeeming and redeemable one.

Both Fielding and Gay would have agreed that puppet shows and ballads, however low they might appear to some carping critics, were preferable to other contemporary theatrical fare because, properly conducted, they could educate the public out of its infatuation with nonsensical entertainments; these native English forms would drive out pernicious foreign influences as well as point out the ludicrousness of many domestic dramatic conventions. Better to enjoy the robust common sense of Punch than the silliness of

French pantomime or the tired dialogue of Cibberian genteel comedy; better to laugh at the absurdities of *Tom Thumb* than to sit poker-faced through the bombast and improbabilities of "modern Tragedy" and believe oneself rationally entertained. Ballad operas, puppet shows, and "laughing" tragedies are, in this respect, provisional forms, meant to clear the stage of the egregious nonsense of incompetent playwrights and profit-minded theater managers, and thus prepare the way for more rational productions. When used by conscious craftsmen like Gay and Fielding, these provisional forms transcend their low, parodic origins and become great art. Great art, however, can be misunderstood and poorly imitated. Fielding wrote *The Grub-Street Opera*, in part, to correct the misunderstandings of the audiences and imitators of *The Beggar's Opera*.

Perhaps the most common misunderstanding aroused by *The Beggar's Opera* concerned its moral purpose. For Gay, Italian opera was a deeply flawed form, both structurally and morally, because its improbable endings did not emerge inevitably from its plots and violated "strict poetical justice";[19] the impending catastrophe would be averted at the last possible moment by ludicrous discoveries and revelations. With all impediments to a happy ending thus removed by operatic fiat, the audience would be sent home after a heart-warming finale of songs, marriages, and dances, as the power of music triumphed over common and artistic sense. What made these closing scenes so ridiculous was that unlike the happy endings of well-made regular comedies, these final reconciliations were seldom foreshadowed and usually entailed a complete reversal of generic expectations. The piece would start off as "a downright deep tragedy"[20] and conclude as a mindless celebration of the author's ingenuity in rescuing his characters from their richly deserved fates. A villain would suddenly repent—or, more likely, be stripped by the author—of his wickedness and marry the woman whose physical and psychological torture had been his delight throughout most of the evening; bitter enemies, now found to be close relations, would embrace and sing a rousing duet on love and friendship. Such coups de théâtre might gratify the spectators' craving for happy endings, but they contributed precious little to their moral edification.

Regular comedy, as Jeremy Collier and his followers rightly

argued, suffered from these same moral deficiencies.[21] A libertine for four and a half acts would wax exemplary in the final scene and marry the rich and virtuous woman. The motivations for these comic endings were often as idiotic as those in Italian opera, a point Fielding illustrates in the absurd denouement of *The Author's Farce*. The major difference was that most of these plays were clearly comic from the start; their comic endings fulfilled generic expectations already present in the work, even if the final moral was ethically dubious. In his regular comedies, Fielding was careful to avoid these moral ambiguities. His heroes may have been libertines at one point in their lives, but by the time the action of the play begins they have thoroughly reformed. The man rewarded at the end is usually a good man of incontrovertible merit as the curtain rises, though he may still have to overcome a few minor infirmities left over from his past. Owen's libertine ways and totally unexpected marriage to Molly at the end of *The Grub-Street Opera* depart from Fielding's usual practice, a departure which, as we shall see, serves as the young playwright's commentary on the moral ambiguities of regular comedy, Italian opera, and, indeed, Gay's own ballad opera.

The debate over the supposed immorality of *The Beggar's Opera* began early in its first season and continued to flare up during the rest of the century. Those who condemned the play found it "shocking" that "an Author [would] bring upon the Stage, as a proper Subject of Laughter and Merriment, a Gang of Highwaymen and Pick-pockets, triumphing in their successful Villainies, and braving the ignominious Death they so justly deserve, with the undaunted Resolution of a Stoical Philosopher."[22] As William Eben Schultz has suggested, some of these attacks—especially that by the Reverend Thomas Herring, a court chaplain and preacher at Lincoln's Inn Chapel, who later rose to the positions of archbishop of York and Canterbury—"may have been made on political grounds," as a defense of Walpole couched in moral and religious language.[23] But, as Schultz adds, most attacks, particularly those made later in the century, cannot be attributed to politics; the "alleged unethical influence" of *The Beggar's Opera* was clearly the issue at stake (p. 229).

If Herring and his crew decried the "unethical influence" of

98

The Beggar's Opera, its defenders—most notably Swift—argued that the author had "by a turn of Humour, entirely new, placed Vice of all Kinds in the strongest and most odious Light; and thereby done eminent service both to Religion and Morality." Swift, however, was Gay's close friend; moreover, he interpreted the attacks on the play as stemming primarily from "servile Attachment to a Party." For him, the moral argument concealed a political motive. Still, the major premises and language of the argument were moral in nature and tone. As a result, the main thrust of Swift's defense is that *The Beggar's Opera* must be judged an "excellent moral performance."[24]

These, then, were the two principal responses to Gay's baffling new play. For Fielding, this mixed reception must have illustrated the potential interpretive pitfalls of scriblerian satire, especially when used in such a highly affective medium as a dramatic representation. While it is clear from the beggar's remarks on "strict poetical justice" at the end of the piece that Gay objects to the false morality of Italian opera, the easy reprieve of Macheath, needed to round off the parody, seems to militate against the moral point the author is making. The beggar, after changing his ending "to comply with the taste of the town," advances that "had the play remained as I first intended, it would have carried a most excellent moral. 'Twould have shown that the lower sort of people have their vices in a degree as well as the rich, and that they are punished for them."[25] But by allowing the player to persuade him to alter his original design, the beggar becomes guilty of the same moral and artistic lapse he condemns so vigorously. The alert spectator or reader might pick up the satirical hints and accept the ending for what it is intended to be, the ethical and aesthetic condemnation of Italian opera, but the brief authorial commentary is apt to be lost on the less perceptive members of the audience who will see only the happy ending and misinterpret, perhaps, the final satirical reprieve as the triumph of vice over virtue.

Such, in brief, was the argument of the more sympathetic contemporary detractors of *The Beggar's Opera*. They recognized the play as a satirical explosion of the absurdities of Italian opera but were disturbed by the manner in which Gay had conducted his satire. In their eyes Gay, in attempting to expose one evil, had perpetrated another. By reducing the high characters of Italian opera to low criminals, Gay had not so much revealed the improbabilities of the genre as glamorized the lives of men and women whose despicable exploits and dreadful deaths had hitherto been confined to clearly moral Newgate biographies and autobiographies. The play's critics feared that "the Agreeableness of the Entertainment, and its being Adapted to the Taste of the Vulgar, and set to easy pleasant Tunes, (which almost everybody can remember,)" would open "the Flood-Gates . . . of the most outragious Enormities."[26] As Benevolus, in a letter to the *London Journal* on 20 April 1728, summarized the case for the "pernicious influence" of *The Beggar's Opera:* "If it be granted that *Dramatick* Performances have any Influence at all on the Minds of the People, (which, I believe was never yet doubted,) it will follow that an Entertainment of this Kind, where almost all the Characters are vicious and criminal, and yet, by the Poignancy of Raillery and Satyr joined to the Charms of Musick, pleasing and delightful; and where the vilest Principles are propagated in the most alluring manner; I say, such an Entertainment must highly tend to corrupt and debauch the Morals of the Nation."[27]

In spite of John Fielding's later assertions to the contrary, it is doubtful that Gay's "Newgate pastoral" has ever had such nefarious consequences.[28] Benevolus's argument merits our attention because it reflects the views of every would-be censor from Plato to our own day. The argument in question is difficult to refute because it is derived from the same premise on which Aristotle bases his theory of drama as mimetic action. "Imitation," Aristotle observes, "is natural to man from childhood; he differs from other animals in that he is the most imitative: the first things he learns come to him through imitation. Then, too, all men take pleasure in imitative representations."[29] Given man's "natural" tendency to imitate the behavior of others, especially when that behavior meets with approval and rewards, there is sufficient warrant, then, for suppressing public entertainments that seem to portray human wickedness in an amiable light. Even if Benevolus and his associates were unable to produce a single verifiable instance of someone's morals being corrupted by the theater, they would still argue that society cannot afford to take the risks, that the very real influence of dramatic performances on the human mind can never be

Imitation

doubted because of the imitative nature of the human animal. For this reason, in order to preserve the common good, dramatic performances must be unequivocally moral.

Although Fielding might not have been so naive as his brother John to believe that *The Beggar's Opera* would actually increase the number of robberies, assaults, and murders, he would have shared his views about the affective power of dramatic performances. Several years later he would begin the first chapter of *Joseph Andrews* with the "trite but true Observation, that Examples work more forcibly on the Mind than Precepts."[30] Such an observation, if true of prose fiction, would apply even more to dramatic presentations, where the impact on the audience is usually unmediated by authorial commentary. To lessen this impact, both Gay and Fielding, in accord with scriblerian practice, introduce an author-within to comment on the action. But, as Fielding recognized, the problem with authorial commentary in the theater is that unless the author-within comments constantly on the internal play, unless he becomes a full-fledged *dramatic* character, as Luckless is in *The Author's Farce* for two acts before the start of his puppet show, his pronouncements are bound to become mere precepts. Gay's mistake in *The Beggar's Opera*, as Fielding saw it, was that he did not keep his beggar on stage throughout the performance. For three hours or so, Gay allows the beggar's character to appeal directly to the sympathies of the spectators. The few minutes the beggar spends on stage explaining Gay's satiric intent cannot, therefore, work as forcibly on the minds of the audience as the lighthearted adventures of Macheath and his fellow rogues. The beggar's dramatic "example," made even more enticing by familiar music, obscures the beggar's satirical precepts. Thus, *The Beggar's Opera* was misunderstood because Gay had failed to control the affective power of his play-within and thereby the response of his audience to it; he had permitted his Newgate pastoral to work its magic and charm virtually unmediated.

Fielding's aim in *The Grub-Street Opera* was to write a ballad opera that would be faithful to the satiric intentions and structure of his scriblerian model without incurring its moral ambiguities. To reach this end, Fielding would have to correct Gay and keep a tighter grip on his audience's response to his moral. He could not, however, rely on the continuous commentary of an author-within because the form, as Gay had conceived it, did not provide for such a sustained explanatory device. One of the reasons *The Author's Farce* could not be considered a real ballad opera was that in it Fielding had allowed the rehearsal structure to predominate. In a ballad opera, authorial commentary is incidental. The "author" should appear only twice: at the beginning to introduce his play and before the conclusion to underscore the improbability of his happy ending. Fielding would follow Gay's original plan, with one significant alteration, in *The Welsh Opera* and find it less than satisfactory. Scriblerus can walk off the stage at the end of his dialogue with the player because he has a "witch to solve" everything.[31] Fielding thus continues Gay's satire on the final discoveries of Italian opera, while at the same time he gently chides his predecessor for writing an ending almost as ludicrous as those he meant to parody. But Fielding realized that a parody of a parody did not offer a satisfactory solution to the serious moral questions raised by *The Beggar's Opera*. Indeed, while Gay's beggar pointedly reminds us of the moral of his play during his second appearance, neither Scriblerus nor his all-solving witch ever mentions the subject. *The Welsh Opera* solves the moral ambiguities of *The Beggar's Opera* by ignoring the moral issue altogether.

The Grub-Street Opera, on the other hand, tackles the moral issue from the start; its apparent scriblerian levity should not obscure this important point. When the player asks Scriblerus about "the plot or design of this opera," the author replies that he has "left . . . out" the former because he has "observed that the plots of our English operas have had no good effect on our audiences," an allusion, perhaps, to the alleged "no good effect" of the "alluring" plot of *The Beggar's Opera* as well as to the moral and artistic lapses of Gay's many imitators, particularly those committed by a young playwright who should have known better than to tie up the loose ends of his ballad opera with a witch. As for the "design," Scriblerus maintains that it is "very deep," that "this opera was writ . . . with a design to instruct the world in oeconomy."[32] He then launches into sixteen lines of doggerel in which he enumerates the many "deep" truths exemplified in his "humble scenes," with the word *teaches*, which opens seven of his eight couplets and appears three times in his last two lines, acting as a sort of refrain in his deliciously simple-minded prefatical "aria." As he had done a few months before in the preface to *The Tragedy of Tragedies*, where he had expounded that "the *Moral* of this excellent Tragedy . . . teaches . . . That Human Happiness is exceeding transient, and, That Death is the certain End of all Men,"[33] Scriblerus once again displays his uncanny grasp for the obvious and the commonplace. Having explicitly apprised his audience of his didactic purpose, Scriblerus Secundus moves "behind the scenes" and, as it happened, out of Fielding's theater. The notorious dramaturgical blockhead had taken his last bow.

Before Scriblerus leaves the stage, however, he focuses his audience's attention on the moral of his piece. His explanation of his purpose may be simple-minded, but it nonetheless points the audience in a moral direction. For Fielding, one of the major omissions of *The Beggar's Opera* lay in the beggar's failure to mention his moral concern in his introduction. It is not until the conclusion of his play, after we have participated vicariously—and, I would argue, approvingly—in the rogueries of his characters, that the author voices his moral aim, an aim he then proceeds to subvert by succumbing to the town's demands for a happy ending. The beggar discovers his "deep design" too late in the game; by then, his viewers have made up their minds about the nature of the entertainment and in most cases, as Gay's detractors claimed and Fielding agreed, missed its moral, because that moral is not explicit enough. Both Gay and Fielding distrusted their audiences' ability to apprehend their "deep designs," but Gay waits too long to disclose his. Fielding adopts a different strategy. We may laugh at the ludicrous manner in which Scriblerus reveals his "deep design," we may chuckle at his solemn insistence on the seriousness of his lighthearted ballad opera, but we must also recognize that Scriblerus's little ditty on the moral of his play is his creator's way of underlining his own moral intent. The explanation offered by Scriblerus must be simple-minded and explicit because Fielding does not wish to be misunderstood: he cannot trust his audience to grasp his "deep design" unaided. Scriblerus is simple-minded, in short, because his *can one buy this ?*

audience is simple-minded. "Deep designs" must be spelled out for a modern audience; Scriblerus, with his penchant for illuminating the obvious, is perfectly suited for this purpose.

Once Scriblerus has "communicate[d] a word or two of [his] design to the audience," he disappears from view.[34] His ballad opera must now carry the burden of its own significance, though the author has alerted us to its possible moral content. At this point, Fielding's experience with the *Tom Thumb* plays proved valuable. In the acting versions of these two plays, as we have seen, Fielding dispenses with the author-within and relies instead on the linguistic absurdities of his characters to convey his satirical intentions. In this respect, the dramatic method of *The Grub-Street Opera* combines elements from Fielding's previous irregular drama. But, unlike *The Author's Farce* and the *Tom Thumb* plays, *The Grub-Street Opera* uses these scriblerian elements not so much to conduct a literary parody as to explore serious moral issues. *The Grub-Street Opera* is not only about the modern "Abuse of Speech" but also about the modern abuse of love. Scriblerus's new ballad opera thus serves as a bridge from the dramatic satire of *The Author's Farce* and the *Tom Thumb* plays to the moral drama of *The Modern Husband*.

The Grub-Street Opera deals with a day in the life of the Apshinken household, especially with the amatory machinations of the family heir, Master Owen, and the fortunes and misfortunes, in love as well as employment, of the family butler, Robin. Master Owen, a fop "in love with womankind,"[35] devotes himself to the pursuit of four women of "strict virtue," while Robin, less than honest in other respects, courts only one of them, Sweetissa, Lady Apshinken's waiting woman. To prevent the union of Robin and Sweetissa, Master Owen "forges" two letters which, he hopes, "will create a jealousy, whereof I may reap the fruit, and Sweetissa's maidenhead may be yet my own" (p. 32). His epistolary ruse succeeds at first, but in the end the forces of "strict virtue" carry the day and the "puny lover" must be satisfied with one woman alone, Molly Apshones, the virtuous daughter of one of his father's tenants. The play concludes with their nuptials and a wedding dance that looks forward to three more marriages: Robin and Sweetissa's, William the coachman and Susan the cook's, and John the groom and Margery the housemaid's.

Such trivial things, then, make up the fabric of Scriblerus's domestic ballad opera. Not only is the playwright foolish but so is his subject matter and so are most of his characters, in particular his two heroes. If Gay's Macheath is the embodiment of attractive virility, Master Owen is a sexual misfit, a veritable Tom Thumb of the boudoir, a half-man who, as Margery punningly observes, must receive a "larger allowance" from his "mamma" before he can live up to his self-proclaimed role as a lady-killer (p. 78). Robin, for his part, is not a dashing highwayman but a petty "rogue" who pilfers his master's liquor and plate on the sly and would rather sing and "scold" his way out of a quarrel than risk bodily injury. While Macheath impresses us with his gallantry, Master Owen and Robin arouse our laughter. Whatever Gay may have intended, Macheath is an appealing character; Master Owen and Robin are bunglers, the objects of our scorn, not of our sympathy and admiration. Even the most feeble-minded spectator can be safely expected to keep his distance from the goings-on at the Apshinken residence. It is difficult, if not impossible, to identify oneself with an impotent idiot or a small-time thief. We may find their escapades amusing, even interesting, but definitely not worthy of our emulation.

Our response to Fielding's two heroines, however, is somewhat more complex. Like Susan and Margery, Molly and Sweetissa are described in the dramatis personae as "women of strict virtue," a phrase that, when applied to the three Apshinken serving girls, is meant to amuse us, as are their constant allusions to their "honour" and "virtue" within the play itself. However chaste waiting-women, cooks, and housemaids might have been in actuality, in literature, especially in the comic drama of the Restoration, they were often portrayed as sexually generous creatures, willing to satisfy the lust of their masters, young or old, for money or dubious proposals of marriage. Indeed, the topos of the easily bedded female servant is a commonplace in the Western comic tradition and would not be worth remarking but for the fact that, owing perhaps to the rising interest in the everyday lives of the lower social orders, several eighteenth-century authors begin to ring changes on it to make a moral point. By anatomizing the thoughts and emotions of the real person behind the stock character, these authors reveal human beings struggling against physical and spiritual dangers, an unpleasant set of circumstances concealed under the veil of the humorous fiction. Defoe's Moll Flanders, for instance, is ruined when she falls for the vague promises of the eldest son of the family that has given her shelter and employment after the death of her nurse. Nine years after Fielding's play, Richardson's Pamela, contrary to type, would hold on to her virtue and find it rewarded in her eventual marriage to the reformed Squire B. In *The Grub-Street Opera*, Fielding also inverts our generic expectations to make a moral point. But, unlike Richardson, who surprises us by his apparent unawareness of the potential humor in his inversion, Fielding wants us to laugh at the *literary* inappropriateness of his below-stairs characters' professions of sexual rectitude. He wants us to laugh, but he also wants us to recognize that their claims are true. The dramatic effectiveness of his play depends on our ability to view its action from these two seemingly contradictory perspectives. Like Scriblerus's poem on the moral of his work, these humorous appeals to virtue and honor demand a double response from the audience to be rightly understood and interpreted.

If Sweetissa's protestations of virtue and honor are both true and amusing, Molly's references to her sexual purity are both serious and intended to be taken as such. While Sweetissa's effusions provoke our laughter by violating our generic expectations, Molly's assertions call for our sober reflection. Unlike Sweetissa's, Molly's virtue is in real danger. Even though we are repeatedly reminded of Master Owen's sexual harmlessness, we are not so sure about his harmlessness in relation to Molly. For one thing, she is thoroughly infatuated with him. Sweetissa, Susan, and Margery are in love with other men and thus protected from Master Owen's blandishments; Molly confronts him directly. When Margery, for example, discovers a momentary weakness for this "fine gentleman," Sweetissa quickly disabuses her friend by declaring that "from such fine gentlemen may my stars deliver me." She then offers the first definition (or redefinition) of "fine gentleman" in the play. Master Owen, Sweetissa believes, may run "after every woman he sees," but "scarce knows what a woman is" because he has "more desire than capacity." Lovers like him—and Sweetissa has "had such lovers!"—can never "stand it out." Sweetissa completes her portrait of these "fine gentlemen" by singing about their presumably compensatory "long pig-tails and shining lace" and observing triumphantly that "there is more in Robin's little finger, than in a beau's whole body" (pp. 35–36). For Sweetissa, "fine gentlemen" come up short in every respect, particularly where it counts most. Given her "virtue," which ought not be equated with sexual naïveté, the sexual innuendos in her observations may be unintentional, but they nonetheless represent the view of the three serving women. This view will eventually be shared by Master Owen himself near the end of the play, after his awkward advances have been snubbed, in three consecutive scenes, by these three "women of strict virtue" and abundant common sense, with Susan offering the most pungent rejoinder to his musical request for a kiss: "A kiss!—a fart" (p. 77).

Molly does not view her lover from this unflattering perspective; she has been totally bamboozled by his foppish show and calls him an "angel" (p. 48). Her father, the repository of solid country virtues and traditional wisdom, is "doubtful" whether the "designs" of this "fine gentleman" are "honourable" (p. 47). For him, Master Owen is a ridiculous but dangerous "baboon" who has "made mischief between several men and their wives" and "seduce[d] the fidler's daughter," though Molly counters this last charge by pointing out that the fiddler "sold his daughter, and gave a receipt for the money" (p. 48). In short, like most fathers and daughters in Restoration and early eighteenth-century comedy, Mr. Apshones and Molly act out the ancient conflict between paternal authority and youthful libido. But in this instance the father is right in his suspicions, as Molly herself soon finds out.

Molly is a curious character. Her name, first of all, links her to Polly Peachum, the heroine of the first and most celebrated ballad opera, though Fielding uses the echo ironically, to underscore how his Molly, despite some superficial resemblances, differs from Gay's Polly. Both girls are torn between their love for a less than admirable man and their duty toward their parents. But while Molly's "strict virtue" prevents her from disobeying her father until the last possible theatrical moment, Polly has married before the beginning of her play. As a result, Polly's "virtue" is never an issue. Indeed, the word appears only once in *The Beggar's Opera*, when the visibly pregnant Lucy upbraids Macheath for having "bilked" her of her "virtue" without "reparation."[36] For Lucy, virtue is to be noted only when it has been lost, a word with no referent, a purely rhetorical gesture; for Polly, who has found "reparation" for her loss of it in her subsequent marriage to Macheath, the word does not even exist. Polly's conflict, therefore, is external, is with her despicable parents over the question of her husband's execution and with her husband over the question of his philandering with Lucy. Molly's struggle is primarily internal, with her virtue and the sexual threat to it, a struggle that is dramatized on stage in her external battles with her father, the champion and projection of her virtue, on the one side, and Master Owen, the libertine rake, on the other. Molly's actions, in other words, are governed by her *moral* conscience—are, in effect, a dramatic allegory of the inner workings of that moral conscience—while Polly's are not. Fielding's heroine, unlike Gay's, thus demands an unequivocally moral response from the audience.

Because Molly's actions reflect her internal struggle with her conscience, her life on stage is characterized by indecision. Like Hamlet, she illustrates how "conscience does make cowards of us all." She cannot decide whether to submit to her father's will or to her lover's. Her only assertive action occurs offstage, when she marries Master Owen, but that assertive action, that declaration of independence from her father's control, may also be interpreted as an act of submission to her lover's desires. In either case, our *dramatic* impression of her character is of a pathetic little creature who lives at the mercy of the two men in her life. Curiously enough, her dramatic helplessness ensures our moral response to her predicament because we recognize that her lack of external assertiveness stems from her "strict" adherence to the virtuous dictates of her conscience, that she is weak in action because she is strong in moral obligation. To understand more fully the reasons for our moral response to Molly, we must return for a moment to the differences in characterization between her and Sweetissa.

Like Molly, Sweetissa imitates the pattern of Gay's heroine. For example, the scene (2.6) in which Sweetissa confronts Susan with the letter that proves the cook's affair with Robin parodies, in its repetition of the word *madam*, the scene (2.13) in which Polly and Lucy "raise a disturbance in the prison" over Macheath.[37] The quarrel between Sweetissa and Susan, however, starts off by focusing our attention on the importance of virtue, while that between Polly and Lucy is strictly about the question of who has the better claim to consider herself the captain's real wife. Again, Gay's women need not mention virtue because they have already parted with it. Both of them—to borrow Susan's words—"have had to do" with Macheath, while Fielding's two servants have not yet ventured "without the precincts of virtue,"[38] and will not "have to do" with their lovers until *after* they are lawfully wedded to them.

Although Sweetissa's debt to Polly goes beyond this "altercative or scolding" scene,[39] the energy she here displays is the one characteristic which identifies her most strongly with her illustrious dramatic ancestor and which at the same time distinguishes her from Molly. That is, in sketching out his two heroines, Fielding seems to have selected the two most salient aspects of Polly's character, her pathetic side and her fighting spirit, and attributed the former to Molly and the latter to Sweetissa. Polly can appear, on the one hand, to be the victim of her parents' and Macheath's cunning; on the other hand, she can show her willingness to assert herself, in her courageous attempts to thwart parental authority and to win the undivided affections of her reluctant husband. In her apparent passivity and weakness, she appeals to our softer passions, to our pity and sympathy; in her tenacity, she evokes our admiration. Like Polly, Sweetissa inspires our allegiance to her cause by her energy, by her ability to act out her will and fight for her man. Unlike Sweetissa and Polly, Molly never gains the upper hand over another character in a "scolding" scene. She cannot afford to dissipate her inner strength in such frivolous displays, in such small victories; she must reserve her energy to sustain her moral conscience. Molly, in short, elicits our sympathy and respect by fighting that most difficult battle of all, with the good and evil within herself.

In isolating Polly's pathetic side and adding an explicitly moral dimension to it, Fielding thus corrects Gay's mistake in *The Beggar's Opera* by carrying his predecessor's criticism of Italian opera one step farther. In her apparent weakness, Gay's Polly recalls the heroines of Italian opera and also the "weeping" female of "she-tragedies" like Rowe's, another one of Gay's satiric targets, soon to be Fielding's as well in *The Covent-Garden Tragedy* (1732), that irreverent send-up of Ambrose Philips's *The Distrest Mother* (1712) written to blast the detractors of *The Modern Husband*.[40] The ludicrous setting and situation of the play—a heroic action conducted by low characters in the seedy underworld of London and Newgate—should have tipped the original audiences that they were watching a parody. Unfortunately, as we have seen, that was not the case because Gay's characters, like those of Italian opera, won their way into the hearts of the spectators by lulling their minds into a soft intellectual sleep; the power of music had undermined the playwright's moral message.[41] As a version of Polly, Molly must also behave like the pathetic heroines of Italian opera and "she-tragedies," but in her overt moral character she differs from all her models. Even though Molly's dramatic life unfolds in a parodic universe—the Apshinken household as both an allegory of the English political scene and an inversion of the aristocratic world of Italian opera—she transcends her initial role as a parody and imitation and becomes a new type of heroine for a new species of explicitly moral ballad opera. In this respect, she resembles the heroines of sentimental or moral comedies like Cibber's and Steele's and looks forward to the moral paragons of Fielding's subsequent drama, particularly to Mrs. Bellamant in *The Modern Husband*.

Thus *The Grub-Street Opera*, while operating on one level as political allegory, can function on another level as an exploration of ethical concepts like love and virtue. This double focus, satiric and romantic, is also present in *The Beggar's Opera*. But Fielding's ballad opera differs from Gay's in its explicit moral emphasis. This is why at the end of *The Grub-Street Opera* Master Owen, after being rejected by all the other eligible women in the play, marries only one woman, the virtuous Molly Apshones. Macheath, though he whispers to Polly that "we were really married," concludes his dramatic career in *The Beggar's Opera* "like the Turk, with his doxies round."[42] Master Owen is also surrounded by the women he has pursued, but they are now to be married to other men. In this fashion, the ending of *The Grub-Street Opera* fixes our eyes and ears on the moral necessity of lawful Christian marriage, while the ending of *The Beggar's Opera*, with its titillating hint of pagan polygamy sung to the rollicking tune of "Lumps of Pudding," undercuts whatever moral the author may have intended. Fielding's next play, *The Modern Husband*, would continue to explore these moral issues in an even more explicit moral framework, as the fairy-tale world of the Apshinken family (witness the last song of the play) would give way to the sordid immoral universe of the Moderns: the young playwright would strive to capture in his dramatic mirror a more true-to-life mimesis of morality.

CHAPTER 6

The Mimesis of Morality:
The Modern Husband

O N NEW YEAR'S Day 1732, nearly six months after the mysterious demise of *The Grub-Street Opera*, *The Lottery* opened at Drury Lane, as Fielding returned to the prestigious house where his first dramatic piece had premiered four years before; the play also marked the beginning of his collaboration with Kitty Clive, for whom he would write such memorable roles as Lettice in *The Intriguing Chambermaid* and Lucy in *An Old Man Taught Wisdom: or, The Virgin Unmask'd* (1735). A charming ballad opera of two scenes—with a third scene depicting the drawing of prizes in the Guildhall added on 10 February 1732—*The Lottery* satirizes yet another pleasure of the town, the yearly lotteries authorized by Parliament to raise funds to alleviate an ever-increasing national debt. As usual with money-making schemes of this sort, these lotteries had become lucrative business for the unscrupulous and the greedy. Stockjobbers and speculators would buy large blocks of tickets and sell them at huge profits. The most common practice of these "jockies of the alley" was known as "horsing": that is, the "letting out [of] tickets for hire at so much a day for any one of the forty days of the drawing." Cheaper than regular tickets, these "horses," often "blank tickets that had already been drawn,"[1] would be hired by "poor wretches"[2] dreaming to better their lot with one lucky turn of the wheel. But even holders of regular tickets stood little chance of winning at a game where "the big prizes had a way of going to someone connected with the Court or to 'a lady in Germany.'"[3] Fielding's heroine, Chloe, is a naive yet cunning girl from the country who, with only a lottery ticket in her pocket, already imagines herself the winner of "Ten Thousand Pound" (prologue to *The Lot-*

tery, p. 267). Her affectations of gentility fool Jack Stocks—who, for his part, pretends to be a lord—into marrying her. With their mutual deception discovered when Chloe's ticket comes up blank, Jack returns his new bride to her old country lover, the sententious Lovemore. The play ends with Lovemore's "profound" observation that his beloved is "not the only person who has been deceived in a lottery" and with a song that equates lotteries with the "world," the "court," the deceitful practices of "doctors and lawyers," and the "stage," "where ten plays are damned, ere one can succeed; / The blanks are so many, the prizes so few" (p. 296).

Judging by its popularity, *The Lottery* was one of those rare theatrical prizes. Fielding's next offering at Drury Lane, *The Modern Husband*, while not exactly a blank with the audience, had a less than enthusiastic reception. Its first performance, on 14 February 1732, was disrupted by hissing, though the play continued to be acted, after some revisions, for thirteen more nights, until 18 March. By contemporary standards, this was a fairly successful showing, especially for a new regular comedy, but for Fielding, the applause accorded his recent acting productions at the Haymarket still ringing in his ears, this modest run must have been disappointing. He had, after all, devoted nearly two years to the making of what he must have deemed his "favourite Child" among his dramatic works.[4] He had, moreover, sent his manuscript to Lady Mary and received encouragement from a woman whose "least approbation," as he wrote to her on 4 September 1730, "will always give me a Pleasure infinitely superior to the loudest Applauses of a theatre." But "the loudest Applauses of a theatre" were what Fielding wanted to hear. A dozen or so performances and the praise of his judicious cousin would prove to be "slight compensation"[5] to an author who—to borrow the words of that other frustrated dramatist, Harry Luckless—had such "great expectations from [his] play" (*The Author's Farce*, p. 10).

The relative failure of *The Modern Husband* has often been attributed to its realistic representation of "a willing cuckold" and "his willing wife" (prologue, p. 10), to the fact that "no audience cares to see actually performed [on stage] all the sordid incidents involved in a husband's sale of his wife in order to pay their gambling debts."[6] This is a fair assessment, but not quite the whole

113

story. The play, as suggested above, was not really a failure, except in the sense that it failed to match the success of Fielding's previous irregular drama. Dramaticus, for example, begins his attack on the piece by granting "the favourable reception *The Modern Husband* has met with from the Town";[7] if the play had flopped, one suspects that Dramaticus and his colleagues at the *Grub-Street Journal* would have made the most of it. Yet *The Modern Husband*, in spite of its fourteen performances, had done less well than Fielding had expected, and it was never revived, another indication of its limited appeal. Its inability to please long stemmed only in part from its sordid subject matter; the age was not that squeamish. "Written on a Model I never yet attempted,"[8] *The Modern Husband* is lacking those essential elements of modern wit—music and visual spectacle—that would have guaranteed it a long run and a place in the repertory. Audiences, both then and now, would rather laugh at a farcical performance of *The Lottery* or *Tom Thumb* than ponder the serious moral questions posed by *The Modern Husband*.[9]

A good place to start our inquiry into Fielding's new dramatic model in *The Modern Husband* is the prologue James Ralph wrote for *The Temple Beau*. "The comic muse," Ralph there proclaims, "in smiles severely gay, / Shall scoff at vice, and laugh its crimes away" (p. 103). We have already noted how these lines describe Fielding's satiric method in *The Temple Beau*, where vicious men and women, though allowed to disturb the order of society, are never real threats to it. We know from the start that these ridiculous characters will be unmasked and beaten at the end, that the good will triumph over these emasculated agents of evil. The satire is mild, benevolent, perhaps a bit facile. We know that life seldom offers the neat patterns of the comic muse, yet we continue to cling to our belief that happy endings are possible, that we can sometimes overcome the weaknesses of our fallible nature. To a lesser extent this belief had also informed the "generous method" of *Rape upon Rape*. *The Modern Husband* questions that belief by depicting a world where evil is all-pervasive, potent, nearly ineradicable.

The presiding muses of the world depicted in *The Modern Husband* are "nature" and "truth" (prologue, p. 9). *Nature* and *truth* are very tricky words, open to distortion and misinterpretation. In the epilogue to *The Temple Beau*, for example, Lady Lucy Pedant upbraids the playwright for "stopping short," for not allowing her and Wilding to make a cuckold of her foolish husband. "Some modern bards," she suggests, would have, "without scruple, the whole thing fulfilled," but the "dullard" who wrote *The Temple Beau*, inspired by a "very modest muse," would "argue that the stage / Was meant t'improve, and not debauch the age" (p. 188). Thus, he denies Lady Lucy her illicit pleasure and, in so doing, ignores the most fundamental tenet of his art: its fidelity to actual human experience. "The stage," she reminds her creator,

> was first designed,
> Such as they are, to represent mankind.
> And, since a poet ought to copy nature,
> A cuckold sure, were not so strange a creature.
> (ibid.)

Given that cuckolds and unfaithful wives exist in the world at large, it follows that they must also appear in the theater, that most faithful mirror of men and manners. In shying away from representing the "fulfillment" of Lady Lucy's guilty passion, the poet and his "very modest muse" have been unfaithful to nature; in contriving "to save [Lady Lucy's] virtue" (ibid.), they have committed artistic adultery.

Lady Lucy's argument for artistic fidelity to nature is sound Aristotelian doctrine and, as we shall soon see, a valid criticism of the dramatic method of *The Temple Beau;* it is also the plea of a libertine couched in the venerable language of classical and neoclassical dramatic theory. For her, nature refers not only to life as it is actually lived but also to a state of being prior to the "imposition" of external laws or moral "improvements." In this natural state, man freely obeys all his natural impulses, and since nature, as Master Owen instructs Molly in *The Grub-Street Opera*, "never prompts us to a real crime" (p. 51), it follows that all the actions of a natural man are beyond moral censure; they cannot be judged by the unnatural rules and constraints of society. By thus redefining nature to mean "license," Master Owen and his fellow libertines seek to replace the moral order of society, in which sexual intercourse between unmarried people is a "crime," with an older, more natural morality—a morality that, upon closer scrutiny, ceases to be moral because it dispenses with all of society's ethical and religious categories of good and evil.

One of the accomplishments of modernity, in Lady Lucy's view, is the adoption in certain fashionable circles of this new morality based on supposedly ancient principles. Society has traditionally frowned upon adultery, but now, as Wilding tells Valentine and Veromil, "cuckoldom is an honour" (*The Temple Beau*, p. 118). The stage, therefore, should not improve its representation of this modern practice with moral judgments for the simple reason that fashionable society no longer condemns it. The author of *The Temple Beau* should copy nature as it is and allow Lady Lucy and Wilding to consummate their intrigue, as they undoubtedly would if they were actual inhabitants of fashionable London or characters in plays by pleasing "modern bards." This is why a playwright who stops short and insists on the moral representation of an amoral world is guilty of a crime against nature and his art, as Lady Lucy perversely redefines *crime*—a word Ralph associates with "vice" in his prologue—to signify her creator's disregard for Aristotle's most celebrated dramatic principle.

Lady Lucy's perverse redefinition of words and her insouciant shuffling of logical and ethical categories are understandable in a character unwilling to abide by the dramatic conventions that define her being in a play by an "improving" author, whose unnatural laws she cannot escape even when she appears to subvert them; she must lodge her complaint in the only part of the play where convention allows characters to break convention, in the epilogue. Behind her selfish plea, however, lies a profound criticism of the dramatic method of *The Temple Beau* and, by implication, of Fielding's other regular plays. Her real intentions notwithstanding, her words call our attention to the gap between life and art in the play we have just seen, in much the same way that the scriblerian strategies of the two versions of *Tom Thumb* reveal the generic incongruities of heroic tragedy. As we have noted before, the world depicted in Fielding's regular plays is not the world of experience, of nature carefully observed and faithfully rendered, but the facetious world of Restoration comedy as reinterpreted and moralized by early eighteenth-century playwrights like Colley Cibber. In this genteel world, cuckolds are God's most amusing creatures, aging coquettes prey on reluctant young sparks, and beaux lisp and wear outlandish clothes and wigs. Men and women who ought to arouse our moral outrage simply make us smile; the final moral is usually a song, a dance, a meaningless cliché. Evil is tamed beyond reprehensibility by dramatic convention.

In this respect, then, Lady Lucy's licentious epilogue may also be read as the expression of Fielding's own dissatisfaction with the outmoded techniques and conventions within which he must work. He also wants to break away from the artificial world of contemporary regular comedy and discover more truthful ways of representing mankind on stage. If Lady Lucy urges the playwright to "copy nature" and thereby dispense with moral improvements, Fielding recognizes that the moral improvements of plays like *The Temple Beau* and *Love in Several Masques*—and, to a lesser extent, *Rape upon Rape*—are ultimately undermined by their unfaithful representation of mankind. In his view, "a poet ought to copy nature" as he finds it in the world around him, with vicious cuckolds, cheating wives, and genuinely good men and women; by keeping a steady eye on nature, he will also teach his audience that neither life nor art is morally neutral. Fashionable London may pretend that traditional rules and conventions no longer apply, but the true poet, that nemesis and antithesis of "modern bards," knows otherwise. It is his task to remind the deluded citizens of the modern world that morality and religion still govern our lives, that no human action escapes unjudged, either by God or by the playwright, that the only true mimesis is the mimesis of morality. This is an ancient lesson usually lost in the final moral platitudes and easy accommodations of genteel comedy.

The model of *The Modern Husband*, then, differs from the model of Fielding's previous regular drama in its serious portrayal of vice. The play accepts the premise that vice is real, a powerful threat to the fragile equilibrium of society, and not a fanciful aberration of human behavior which laughter can effortlessly scoff away. Virtue still triumphs at the end, as it must in comedy, but this final victory is never a foregone conclusion. In *The Modern Husband*, virtue wins out only after struggling with a most formidable foe, and its most effective weapon in this struggle is not laughter but Mrs. Bellamant's love for her adulterous husband.

117

Love between husbands and wives and the violations of that love define the thematic boundaries of *The Modern Husband;* these thematic boundaries are defined, in turn, by card games, sexual embraces, mirrors, and monsters. Monsters deserve our attention first because Mr. Bellamant introduces them at the beginning, in the prologue. It is appropriate that he do so because, as an essentially good man who cheats on his wife, he provides the nexus between the two categories of characters—monsters and nonmonsters—which make up the play's dramatis personae. He uses the word twice, first to classify the author's irregular drama, those "unshaped monsters of a wanton brain," and then to pass judgment, from the perspective of traditional dramatic theory, on the protagonists of the piece: "A pair of monsters most entirely new!" (p. 9). A "willing cuckold" and "his willing wife," if truthfully depicted, are bound to appear as monsters, especially to audiences nurtured on the decorous niceties of regular comedy. But such monsters not only exist in society; their vicious practices are condoned and rewarded by law: a "willing cuckold" can collect a tidy sum from a timely "discovery." [10] The label "monsters," therefore, is ironic, a dodge for those who dislike seeing an ugly social truth faithfully rendered on the stage; it is also a word that categorizes all the creatures and creations of modernity, in life as well as in the theater, from Tom Thumb to Mrs. Modern. Fielding's double use of the word *monsters* suggests that he is not so much condemning his irregular drama as indicating that his new play continues to fight the war against the pleasures of the town, a war he had openly declared in *The Author's Farce,* in a more sober and overtly moral fashion. As we finish hearing or reading the prologue to *The Modern Husband,* we realize that a "willing cuckold" and "his willing wife" are the "monsters" shaped by the "wanton brain" of fashionable society, and that it is the office of the playwright to "draw the town" (p. 10) in all its viciousness, even if he must break a few dramatic conventions and risk offending the "carping" critics of the *Grub-Street Journal.* [11]

Fielding's break with traditional dramatic conventions in *The Modern Husband* has been acknowledged by every student of the play, from Dramaticus to John Loftis. [12] Yet the nature of that break has remained elusive because the play has seldom been examined sympathetically or on its own terms as a dramatic work. The carp-ing critics of the *Grub-Street Journal*, for instance, blasted the author for his monstrous assault on decency, taste, and sense, not to men-tion his scandalous contempt for dramatic rules. Modern scholars have disagreed with this harsh assessment and praised Fielding for his realism and morality, but cannot fully accept that his new model works as drama. Cross, for example, remarks that "what [Fielding] had really produced, though perhaps he was not aware of it, was a novel in dramatic form running through five Acts to eighty-odd pages of prose."[13] I must confess that I cannot picture "a novel in dramatic form" anymore than I can envisage an opera in pantomime. To be sure, Fielding's concerns in *The Modern Hus-band* are similar to the concerns of contemporary writers of prose fiction like Defoe and, to look forward a few years, Samuel Rich-ardson. Indeed, nineteen years later, Fielding himself would model the marital difficulties of Captain Booth and Amelia on those of Mr. and Mrs. Bellamant. But these similarities in subject matter cannot be regarded as evidence that early eighteenth-century drama was becoming novellike; one isolated feature does not a genre make. The point is obvious and need not be belabored. A work of litera-ture which consists of scenes and dialogue and which is meant to be acted by actors before an audience has traditionally been consid-ered a play. This may be a simple-minded argument for establish-ing that *The Modern Husband* is a play and not "a novel in dramatic form"—a phrase that ultimately contradicts itself by making a spe-cious distinction between form and content—but it has the virtue of reaching its conclusion without contradicting the physical evi-dence or affronting common sense.

If we begin by granting that *The Modern Husband* is indeed a play, we can then proceed to determine the extent of its departure from Restoration and eighteenth-century dramatic patterns. When Fielding confided to Lady Mary that his play had been "written on a Model I never yet attempted," he no doubt meant to emphasize the originality of his new dramatic design. But the model of *The Modern Husband* was not exactly unattempted; it had come about as a result of Fielding's experiments with irregular forms. Like *The Author's Farce*, *The Modern Husband* breaks the conventions of tradi-tional regular comedy by presenting these conventions in a context

Violation
of
expectation

that calls attention to their status *as* conventions. Both plays start off by pretending to be regular comedies, thus raising certain generic expectations, that are then not so much unfulfilled as fulfilled in strange new ways. Luckless begins as the hero of a romantic comedy and, as expected, marries his beloved Harriot at the end. But, in order to do so, he must become a puppet master and the king of a ludicrously rich kingdom; while his future bride, who must now claim royal blood to marry her suitor, finds that royalty in the improbable world of *The Author's Farce* carries the unusual burden of kinship to puppets. This, to say the least, is a bizarre way to conclude a romantic comedy, and, in fact, even at this point, the piece is not over; the metamorphoses continue as an epilogue-in-process is spoken by an actress whose identity fluctuates from woman to cat, from cat to woman, and so on, ad infinitum et ad absurdum. *The Modern Husband* does not play these facetious games with dramatic perspective and dramatic genre; but the games it does play are decidedly scriblerian.

From its opening scenes, *The Modern Husband* declares itself a play about interpretation, judgment, and games—specifically, card games.[14] As the curtain rises, Mrs. Modern is at her morning toilet, with her servant Lately attending. Like the actress impersonating Mrs. Modern, the character Mrs. Modern cannot face her daily audience until she is properly dressed for the part, and though Lately assures her that she is "drest," Mrs. Modern thinks herself "frightfully drest" and would begin her morning ritual "all again . . . if it were not too late" (1.1 [13]).[15] But it is too late; the performance must start. It is also too late because Mrs. Modern does not have any money,[16] and one must have money to be a successful player in her world. Mrs. Modern is "frightfully drest": her mirror tells her so, even if Lately disagrees. Mrs. Modern is concerned with appearances; she is also an avid player of card games, as testified by the nearly interminable list of engagements in her "Quadrille-book" (1.2 [14]).

Card games and mirrors—in addition to monsters—are the controlling images, the central metaphors, of the world represented in *The Modern Husband*. Mirrors tell us about our appearance, whether that appearance matches the reality we wish to project. Mirrors, in *The Modern Husband*, are metaphorical: characters serve as mirrors for other characters, reflecting on appearances, passing judgments on actions. Lately is that other mirror into which Mrs. Modern gazes every morning, to confirm her looks and prejudices, though throughout the play Lately acts as a talking mirror with a mind almost all of her own (eventually, of course, she must come around to her employer's view of the world). Mr. Bellamant is, according to his wife, "the most complaisant man in the world," who compliments her every morning on her dress and appearance, thus contradicting the unfavorable verdict of the town and the practice of "most husbands" who, in Mrs. Bellamant's view, "are like a plain-dealing looking-glass, which sullies all the compliments we have received abroad by assuring us we do not deserve 'em" (2.1 [26]). Mrs. Bellamant is right, though she does not know it. Her husband's compliments may be sincere, but they also conceal his guilt. He is not really a "plain-dealing looking-glass"; he is unfaithful to his wife. Plain dealing—in words, in cards, in love—defines the moral structure of *The Modern Husband*.

Mirrors, in the abstract, are plain dealers, faithful reflectors of reality. In practice, however, mirrors distort because their reflections are observed and interpreted by human beings, and human beings are notoriously deficient judges of human character and actions. In the theater, as Fielding well understood, audiences often misinterpret the action mirrored onstage, even though it has already been interpreted by the author. In *The Modern Husband* Fielding tries to make sure that his audience will interpret correctly by adapting the author-within technique of his irregular drama and using his characters, as internal mirrors, to reflect and pass judgment on each other's actions. These reflections and judgments are sometimes wrong and sometimes on the button, but in both cases they point the audience in the right direction; in doing so, they also underscore the differences between Fielding's new play and traditional regular comedy. Mr. Bellamant, for example, believes that Lord Richly is the typical harmless fop of Restoration comedy—a perception reinforced for the original Drury Lane audiences by the fact that Colley Cibber, the stage fop par excellence of the age, played the part. Mr. Bellamant theorizes that Lord Richly is composed of "a great deal of affectation" and that "he oftener injures women in their fame, than in their persons" (2.6 [35]). But, as his repugnant affair with Mrs. Modern illustrates, Lord Richly is a dangerous man, an agent of the "devil" (p. 46) who will "tempt" (p. 33) Mrs. Bellamant as he has tempted other women. Mr. Bellamant does not understand that he and Lord Richly are characters in a new play, where the old dramatic conventions no longer apply; Lord Richly is not another version of the impotent Master Owen, the dim-witted Rattle (also played by Cibber) of *Love in Several Masques*, or the bungling Sir Novelty Fashion—all worthy imitators of that "pattern of modern foppery," Etherege's Sir Fopling Flutter[17]—but a potent, deviously scheming violator of the marriage bed. Mr. Bellamant's misunderstanding, or misreading, of Lord Richly's character thus makes a point about the difficulties of arriving at correct moral evaluations, both in life and in the theater, as well as about the moral purpose of the new model of *The Modern Husband*.

Like *The Author's Farce*, then, *The Modern Husband* relies on a dramatic model that consists both of action and of constant interpretation of that action; and the action and the interpretation, given the potentially ambiguous subject matter of the play, must be unequivocally moral. Even when the moral of a scene is clear, as in the scenes depicting Lord Richly's levee, we must still have the elucidations of Captain Bravemore and Captain Merit (p. 22), not to mention Lord Richly's own capping aphorism that "a levee is the paradise of fools" (p. 25). No action, in short, can go uninterpreted, and, as a result, characters in *The Modern Husband*, like characters in *The Author's Farce, Pasquin*, and *The Historical Register*, are always aware that they are acting, that there is an audience, either on stage or in the pit and gallery, for whom their performances will have meaning. *The Modern Husband* achieves its realism, its fidelity to nature and truth not so much by representing real people and real human situations, though it does this to a considerable extent, as by constantly reminding its viewers that they are watching a play. That is, even though *The Modern Husband*, unlike genteel comedies, goes a long way in its unflinching depiction of sordid social fact— something that would not be attempted again in European theater until Ibsen's drama of social realism—it does not aim completely to knock down the barriers between art and life. In fact, as far as Fielding is concerned, the more aware his spectators are that they are watching a play, the better, because they are then less likely to identify with the action unfolding on stage and more apt to attempt to determine what that action is supposed to *mean*. In *The Modern Husband* the fourth wall never entirely disappears because Fielding, like Brecht and unlike Ibsen, firmly believes that drama is at its most realistic only when it calls attention to its own theatricality. This is why "all the sordid incidents involved in a husband's sale of his wife" are not actually performed in *The Modern Husband*, as Cross would have it, but staged in terms of metaphors that heighten the viewer's awareness of the play as a theatrical performance.

Of all the metaphors Fielding uses in *The Modern Husband*, none is so successful in highlighting the theatricality of the piece as the card games his characters are constantly playing or, as in the case of Emilia and Gaywit, refusing to play. With every reference to card games, the audience is reminded that it is looking at players: players of card games, players of marital (or premarital or extramarital) games, players of the play called *The Modern Husband*. The analogy between card games and marriage is explicitly made by Mrs. Modern in the fourth scene of the first act, after the audience has seen her dressing up for that day's performance, heard three weeks' worth of engagements read out of her Quadrille-book, and been told, again by Mrs. Modern, that a certain Mrs. Worthy "plays at Quadrille worse than she dresses" (1.3 [15]). Mrs. Modern tells her "wretch" of a husband that "the very worst of Quadrille is, one cannot cheat without a partner" (p. 16), which is not only true of quadrille, but also of their peculiarly gamelike matrimonial arrangement.

Quadrille is a game for four players, and *The Modern Husband* is a play about the marital games of four couples. Mr. and Mrs. Modern have run out of money because Mrs. Modern, as her husband, borrowing a theatrical phrase, says, does "not manage Lord Richly right" (ibid.). Mr. and Mrs. Bellamant are happily married, except for the fact that they, too, are running out of money and Mr. Bellamant is being "managed" by Mrs. Modern. Emilia and Gaywit, the romantic couple from conventional comedy, have not yet married but will do so as soon as they discover their love for each other and clear up their monetary difficulties. Mr. Gaywit, it must be added, has also fallen for the charms of Mrs. Modern, principally for the sake of Mr. Bellamant's moral quatrain at the end of the play (p. 96), in which Mr. Bellamant's sexual indiscretion acts as a cautionary tale for young men with libertine tendencies. Finally, Captain Bellamant and Lady Charlotte Gaywit, the empty-headed fop and the coquette of genteel comedies, realize that "two people" who "think alike . . . act alike . . . and are very much alike in the face" (p. 78) have no choice but to marry; Captain Bellamant and his bride-to-be are perfect mirrors of each other, a parodic version of Emilia and Gaywit, of Mr. and Mrs. Bellamant, and understudies for Mr. and Mrs. Modern. In addition, they are the only two characters in the play who attempt to speak in the witty accents of Restoration comedy, but, because of their less than agile intellects, their "wit-traps" fail to work; moderns ought to speak plainly or at least in plain prose.

Quadrille is a game for four players, for two partners against two partners, and, therefore, not conducive to the kind of intimacy needed for a successful seduction. A single man with designs on another man's wife does not play quadrille; he plays the more intimate, one-on-one game known as picquet. As one would suspect, Lord Richly is a consummate picquet player. By defeating Mrs. Modern at picquet—after she, in Lady Charlotte's flamboyant phrasing, has "won all the world" at hazard (p. 42)—he manages to persuade her to "contrive . . . a meeting between me and Mrs. Bellamant, at your house" (3.1 [44]). In order to ensure his success at that meeting, Lord Richly plays picquet with Mrs. Bellamant at her house and loses "six parties successively" (3.10 [54]). Mrs. Bellamant is "confident . . . that he has lost the last party designedly" and begins to sense, in a grim pun, that "he certainly hath a design on me" (3.11 [55]). He has left a hundred pound note with her, or, as Mrs. Modern later puts it, "a hundred friends in the garrison" (4.2 [62]). But Lord Richly's skill in card games does not help him in this instance. Mrs. Bellamant remains faithful to her husband, and it is this same hundred pound note—a particularly modern variation on the recognition token of traditional comedy and romance—that brings about the discovery of Mr. Bellamant's infidelity (4.9 [73]) and his subsequent forgiveness by his loving wife (4.10 [75]). The picquet match between Lord Richly and Mrs. Bellamant, which takes place near the structural center of the play, is the last card game in *The Modern Husband;* it is also the beginning of marital reconciliation, of the unraveling of the play's entangled marriage games, as each player finds his or her true partner in love, and the Moderns, all their games played out, prepare to leave for the country.

But the play is not over. As the curtain falls on the last scene, Mrs. Modern steps forward, and, like Lady Lucy in her epilogue, denounces the "dull poetic sentence" that dictates that she "in lonely woods . . . must pursue repentance" (p. 100). "Hang the stupid Bard!—I'll stay in town"—with these defiant words, Mrs. Modern finally stalks off the stage, thus showing that, to the last and even beyond, she is a poor player who refuses to play by the rules of the game.

In the four years between the last performance of *The Modern Husband* and the opening night of *Pasquin*, Fielding produced nine new plays, revised and expanded *The Author's Farce*, and had the pleasure of seeing many of his earlier efforts in revivals.[18] He continued to be attacked by the *Grub-Street Journal*, and, like any other playwright, had his share of successes (*The Old Debauchees, The Mock-Doctor, The Miser, An Old Man Taught Wisdom*) and disasters (*The Covent-Garden Tragedy* and *The Universal Gallant*). But viewed from the perspective of his dramatic development, these were relatively lean years. With the possible exception of *The Covent-Garden Tragedy*, which intensifies the parodic techniques of *Tom Thumb* by concentrating on one single target,[19] none of his new plays can be considered dramatically significant. His most popular plays during these years, his imitations and adaptations of Molière, are important not because of formal and thematic innovations, the hallmarks of his career up to *The Modern Husband*, but because of their debt to Molière and the histrionic talents of Kitty Clive.

Yet there were a few harbingers of things to come. In January 1734, at the height of the theatrical war between Theophilus Cibber and John Highmore, Fielding offered the beleaguered manager and actors of Drury Lane an up-to-date version of *The Author's Farce* in which he sharpened the personal satire against the Cibbers and, now that the elder Cibber had been elected poet laureate, the political implications as well.[20] And, three months later, in April, he took a "Comedy . . . begun at Leyden in the year 1728,"[21] added to it a few scenes satirizing political elections, and returned to the Little Theatre in the Haymarket for the first time since the troubles over *The Grub-Street Opera*. As if to underscore the connection between his ill-fated ballad opera and his new play, Fielding introduced *Don Quixote in England* to his audience with a scriblerian dialogue between manager and author. More important, on 18 April, when the play was published, it was dedicated to Lord Chesterfield. Fielding had not only returned to the scene of his popular acting plays; he had also publicly announced that his pen now belonged to the Opposition.[22] In the next two years, before the Licensing Act put the Great Mogul and his company out of business, Fielding would write and direct his two most controversial and successful irregular plays, *Pasquin* and *The Historical Register for the Year 1736*. Politics could no longer be kept out of the playhouse, and the young dramatist with partisan zeal began to compose brilliant sketches for what proved to be the last chapter of his dramatic career.

CHAPTER 7

The Politics of the Playhouse: *Pasquin* and *The Historical Register for the Year 1736*

FIELDING'S LAST FIVE plays before the Licensing Act—*Pasquin*, *Tumble-Down Dick*, *Eurydice*, *The Historical Register for the Year 1736*, and *Eurydice Hiss'd*—were written on the model of *The Author's Farce*. All five plays rely on the rehearsal structure and techniques of his first irregular piece; all five continue his satire on the pleasures of the town; all five, unlike their prototype, deal specifically with politics. Politics had never been totally absent from Fielding's drama; no dramatist of the 1730s, if he wished to be truthful to nature, could have avoided the most prominent concern of the age. But in the 1730 version of *The Author's Farce*, for instance, or in the *Tom Thumb* plays, politics are referred to only by isolated allusions. One of these allusions, however, deserves notice. In *The Author's Farce* Witmore attributes the contemporary decline in taste to "party and prejudice" (p. 16). Although Witmore's observation is a commonplace—the type of blanket indictment of modernity ridiculed in *The Historical Register* in the first player's notion of drama as a "humming deal of satire"[1]—it nonetheless marks the first explicit connection in Fielding's plays between theatrical and political spheres. Fielding would elaborate on this connection in *The Welsh Opera*, where the seemingly innocuous transactions of the Apshinkens and their servants point clearly in the direction of the royal family and the ministry. Dramatic actions thus become analogies for political actions, as actors on one stage remind the audience of actors on another stage.

127

In his last plays—particularly in *The Historical Register* and *Eurydice Hiss'd*—Fielding would carry this process of dramatic analogy to its logical conclusion and represent political events, not in terms of the humorous mishaps of a Welsh family, but in terms of the theater itself. Medley, the author of a play titled *The Historical Register*, enlightens the critic Sourwit about "how [his] political is connected with [his] theatrical": "When my politics come to a farce, they very naturally lead to the playhouse where, let me tell you, there are some politicians too, where there is lying, flattering, dissembling, promising, deceiving, and undermining, as well as in any court in Christendom."[2] This natural connection between the politics of the playhouse and the politics of Walpole's England, between affairs of stage and affairs of state, caused Fielding to return to the scriblerian strategies of his first irregular play with renewed interest and with the conviction that he could discover new dramatic possibilities in the rehearsal of the pleasures of the town.

One of the lessons Fielding had learned while rehearsing the pleasures of the town in *The Author's Farce* had been that contemporary amusements are virtually interchangeable, that Don Tragedio's professions of linguistic excellence, to select a familiar example, "very naturally lead" to the equally extravagant claims of Sir Farcical, and these, in turn, lead to those of Dr. Orator, and so on. The protean nature of modern diversions is, therefore, reflected in the play's dizzying movement from comedy to farce to puppet show, in its fluid pageant of personified literary genres, now no longer what they once were, in its climactic confusion of characters and puppets. These strange metamorphoses continue into the epilogue, as the play ends by projecting itself into a chaotic future where no end exists, where flux reigns supreme. When Fielding in *Tom Thumb* wrestles with this modern Proteus and tries to hold him down to one single shape, he finds that the creature keeps changing, that the satiric object refuses to be objectified, that one pleasure of the town cannot be invoked without conjuring up all others. This apparent catastrophe is actually a gain: the satirist's task is simplified once he recognizes that one modern aberration inevitably calls to mind the whole context of modernity. Thus, in *The Modern Husband* Fielding can represent the Moderns' sordid practices metaphorically, with the play's ludic structure mirroring the moral frivolity of fashionable London, where human actions, from courtship to marriage to playgoing, are reduced to, and interpreted as, games. *The Modern Husband,* in short, discovers the quintessence of modernity, its deep ludic structure, and embodies it in a complex dramatic metaphor. The dramatic metaphor of Fielding's last plays draws its power from the quintessential connections between the political and the theatrical.

The word *quintessence* belongs to Medley. The prologue to his new play is an "Ode to the New Year," a hodgepodge of clichés and imbecilities ("the sun shall rise," "the moon shall be bright," etc.) extracted from the sublime effusions lovingly crafted by the poet laureate to commemorate the king's birthday and New Year's Day.[3] When the singers have finished singing his ode, Medley exclaims that "that's the very quintessence and cream of all the odes I have seen for several years" (p. 17). That is, Medley has studied contemporary odes long and hard, as Fielding had studied regular comedy before writing *Love in Several Masques,* and discovered their deep structure. Hence he can compose an ode that is the "quintessence"—the Platonic Idea, as it were—of all odes written within recent memory, an ode which not only refers to all Cibberian odes but also an ode to which, by virtue of the modern principle of *hysteron proteron* so learnedly enunciated in Scriblerus's preface to *The Tragedy of Tragedies* (pp. 42–43), all Cibberian odes can now refer. The concept of quintessence is the cornerstone of Medley's dramatic method in *The Historical Register,* and of Fielding's model both in *Pasquin,* where Sneerwell calls it "Emblematical,"[4] and in *The Historical Register for the Year 1736,* which "is writ," in Medley's words, "in allegory" (p. 27).

Pasquin opened on 5 March 1736 and ran, with few interruptions, for fifty-nine nights; its popularity carried over into the following season, when another production by the Great Mogul's Company of Comedians, *The Historical Register for the Year 1736,* became the town's favorite entertainment.[5] Praise for Fielding's "Dramatick SATIRE *on the* TIMES" was nearly unanimous,[6] though there were some dissenting voices, most notably that of Marforio in the *Grub-Street Journal.*[7] The object of all this attention was a five-act "REHEARSAL of TWO PLAYS, *viz.* A COMEDY call'd, THE ELECTION; And a TRAGEDY call'd, The LIFE and DEATH of COMMON-SENSE" (title page), the joke presumably being that, in order to fill up a regular five-act structure, one needed to act both a modern comedy and a modern tragedy. Each play-within is rehearsed in its entirety, with each rehearsal taking up approximately two and a half acts of *Pasquin*. The comedy is regular; the tragedy, on the other hand, is irregular, consisting of only three acts. As Fustian explains to Sneerwell, his piece may be "immethodical," but he has an excellent reason for contravening the most revered Aristotelian rule of them all: "I spun it [his tragedy] out as long as I could keep *Common-Sense* alive; ay, or even her Ghost" (4 [38]). Unlike the surprisingly commonsensical Fustian, most modern tragedians follow the advice of critics like Sneerwell and thereby reduce all dramatic art to Aristotelian or Horatian clichés; such blind devotion to convention for the sake of convention inevitably gives rise to five-act plays on topics that merit, at best, only three—or, what is often closer to the truth, none whatsoever. In this respect, Fustian's name, like Trapwit's, actually belies his understanding of the craft he practices. Unlike the wholly inept dramatic hacks ridiculed in rehearsal plays from Buckingham onward, both Fustian and Trapwit, in spite of some regrettable lapses, know what they are doing most of the time. Neither Fustian's tragedy nor Trapwit's comedy can be said to resemble the typically bad play-within of the traditional rehearsal; neither play is the primary object of Fielding's satire in *Pasquin*. Instead, each one of these miniature sketches presents, within its reduced frame, a "Dramatick SATIRE *on the* TIMES," as Fielding discovers in Fustian and Trapwit two unlikely allies in his war against the pleasures of the town.

The pleasures of the town ridiculed in Trapwit's play are explicitly political, centering around a disputed election in a country borough. In fact, Trapwit's comedy is, in many ways, a rewriting of Fielding's own *Don Quixote in England*. As in the earlier play, the political satire is general and even-handed: Trapwit demonstrates that all politicians, whether "Whig and Tory; Or Court and Country Party" (1 [5]), are equally corrupt. The quintessential truth about modern elections, Trapwit and Fielding suggest, is that both parties will "Bribe away with Right and Left" (p. 7), though some candidates, like Sir Harry, do their bribing indirectly, as Trapwit

130

explains, while others, like Lord Place, do so more directly, but because of the forgetfulness of the prop man, do so without money (p. 8). The stage, in short, is such a faithful mirror of "nature" (Trapwit's word) that even when it appears to fail in its representation of political corruption, it actually manages to be more accurate than the beleaguered playwright suspects. As Fustian puts it, "The Actor has out-done the Author; this Bribing with an empty Hand is quite in the Character of a Courtier" (ibid.). Fustian is wrong to exult in his colleague's apparent failure: Trapwit has written a scene in which either outcome would be true to nature; the prop man, by his carelessness, has unwittingly turned a good scene into an even better one. Trapwit, after all, knows that "the Art of a Writer . . . is, to diversifie his Matter, and do the same thing several ways" (ibid.). That "same thing," variously represented, is the quintessential corruption of modern political life; and that political quintessence cannot be better captured than in a playhouse that is quintessentially in disarray and in political turmoil. Men like Rich and the Cibbers, through their greed and political machinations, have turned the theater into a perfect mirror of the times; a satirist need be only passingly competent to score points off such easy targets.

If Trapwit's comedy, whatever its demerits, faithfully captures the quintessence of modern politics by satirizing that most quintessential of political transactions, the election, Fustian's tragedy carries the process of quintessential representation one step farther by dramatizing the underlying pattern that serves as the metaphorical link between stage and state actions. That link, for Fustian and Fielding, can be found in the modern disregard for traditional moral and intellectual imperatives, or, in Fustian's "Emblematical" terms, in the modern worship of Queen Ignorance and disdain for Queen Common-Sense. But even while staging his dramatic emblem for the decline of civilization as he knew it, Fielding introduces some additional complications. His original audiences at the Haymarket would have noted that the actress playing Queen Common-Sense had acted the part of Mrs. Mayoress in Trapwit's comedy. This doubling of parts would have planted a seed of suspicion in the audience's collective mind: how can we trust a deity

131

one has just seen in the role of a very earthly, very foolish old woman? Queen Common-Sense seems admirable enough, but the *visual* evidence appears to undermine her admirable character. This is, of course, the problem with the modern world: one can never be sure whether the appearance corresponds to reality, whether one is being deluded by a performance, whether Queen Common-Sense, as in the dedication the poet vows to write (5 [49]), is Queen Ignorance in disguise. Folly reveals and conceals itself under several masks.

What *Pasquin* does, in short, by offering us these fleeting moments of uneasy recognition, by constantly exposing the underlying mechanism of the theatrical illusion, is to emphasize the importance and wisdom of observing life as though it were a theatrical performance—a quintessential point Fielding raises over and over in his dramatic career, beginning with the opening scene of *Love in Several Masques* and the play's subsequent concern with the reading of acting. We may note in the playhouse that one actor or actress is playing several parts, that life on stage is performance, but in life, because we are so caught up in our own performances, we seldom recognize the histrionic basis of all human behavior. This is why we are easily deceived by the actions of others, even though, as Fielding would later remark, we tend to speak of human activities in the language of the stage.[8] But this stage language, like most metaphorical language—as illustrated by the characters in *Tom Thumb* and *The Tragedy of Tragedies*—is often used without awareness of the underlying metaphor, without a thought about its implications and consequences. We all know that the world is a stage, but through mindless repetition we no longer understand what the analogy between world and stage involves, what it can teach us about our behavior and the behavior of others. In *Pasquin* Fielding revitalizes this theatrical commonplace by dramatizing, in "Emblematical" detail, the connections between life as acted on stage and life as acted in the world. And the world, for Fielding and his contemporaries, pullulated with political meaning. *Pasquin* may not have been as "bitterly satiric [as] other political satires of the time,"[9] but the lessons it taught its audience, because taught with such subtlety and such apparent good nature, must have

132

deeply disturbed those in power. Any play that seeks to heighten the perceptions of its audience, that challenges its viewers to read the world with histrionic detachment, makes an emphatic political statement. *The Historical Register for the Year 1736* would differ from *Pasquin* in directing that political statement, explicitly and unequivocally, at Walpole and his ministers, in inviting its spectators and readers to find specific partisan applications in its transparent political allegory.

The unmistakable anti-Walpole applications of the dramatic allegory of *The Historical Register* have often been cited—at least since Colley Cibber's celebrated pronouncement on the subject in his irrepressible *Apology for His Life* (1740)—as one of the main factors contributing to the passage of the Licensing Act. While it would be difficult to establish that *The Historical Register* was one of the principal protagonists in this dramatic tragedy—the law, after all, was already on the books and efforts to enforce it had begun as early as 1735—it is almost as difficult to deny it its prominent role.[10] The play, as any reader can plainly see, was intended to offend: "He who maketh any wrong application thereof," as Fielding himself devilishly suggests in his dedication to the public, "might as well mistake the name of Thomas for John, or Old Nick for Old Bob" (p. 8). Indeed, even though Fielding does not develop the diabolical connections of Walpole and his minions with the thoroughness that the dedication might lead us to expect, there is a scene (pp. 36–37) in which these connections are perhaps suggested through Miltonic and biblical allusions. Pistol, Theophilus Cibber's dramatic alter ego, storms the stage and speaks to the mob of his part in the "glorious enterprise," a reference to the well-known spat between his wife Susanna and Kitty Clive over the role of Polly; Satan speaks to his cohorts of their "Glorious Enterprise" in his first speech in *Paradise Lost* (1.89). The citizens then express their sentiments on Cibber's "successless" mission with a theatrical hiss. "That hiss," Pistol tells his audience,

> speaks their assent.
> Such was the hiss that spoke the great applause
> Our mighty father met with when he brought
> His *Riddle* on the stage.

133

When Satan returns to Hell, "successful beyond hope" (463), after carrying out his temptation of Eve, his companions hiss their approval:

> So having said, a while he stood, expecting
> Their universal shout and high applause
> To fill his ear, when contrary he hears
> On all sides, from innumerable tongues
> A dismal universal hiss, the sound
> Of public scorn.
>
> (10.504-9)

Finally, after Cibber/Pistol finishes his oration, Medley dismisses him with "Get thee gone," a possible echo of Christ's words to Satan in the wilderness, "Get thee hence" (Matthew 4:10) and "Get thee behind me" (Luke 4:8).[11] These hits at the Cibbers, together with Fielding's usual roasting of beaux, auctions, and other inhabitants and pleasures of Old England, constitute the brilliant dramatic fabric of the Great Mogul's most exuberant acting play.[12]

As a critical term, _exuberance_ does not seem promising, yet it would be hard to come up with a word that better describes Fielding's dramatic art. *Love in Several Masques* and *The Temple Beau* offer a compendium of clichés borrowed from Restoration and early eighteenth-century comedy, but, as I have suggested at the beginning of this study, Fielding's precocious confidence in his dramatic powers breathes new life into the old conventions. In *The Author's Farce* Fielding's energy and exuberance are omnipresent: the play refuses to hold still; it holds a mirror up to its maker's hyperactive imagination. *The Author's Farce* is thus always threatening to run out of control, to become one with the chaos it must hold at bay to make its satiric statement. There is, in other words, more than a hint of immaturity lurking in the play's brilliant execution. The modern world may be an amorphous heap, but art, if it is to perform its didactic function, must erect boundaries to stave off dissolution. Art must make a statement: it must not merely record; it must also interpret and organize. In *The Author's Farce* Fielding senses that he is letting his exuberance control his art, and, as a result, he feels that he must apologize for what he is doing.

In *The Historical Register* there are no apologies, no intimations of uneasiness, because Fielding has discovered a new way of representing the pleasures of the town. In *The Author's Farce* Fielding is constantly insinuating that he is not the real author of Luckless's puppet show; indeed, even Luckless himself tries to disown his own work. As we sit in the theater, we are asked to believe that this particular puppet show is a parody, that there is a satiric purpose to all this nonsense. The play, therefore, breaks up into a foreground of commentary and a background of modern diversions, into the frame provided by the "reading" romantic comedy and the "acting" puppet show that refuses to be contained within that conventional frame. Like the *Tom Thumb* plays, *The Author's Farce* aims to convey its satiric intent to its viewers by making them aware of the discontinuities in its representation. *The Historical Register* and *Pasquin*, on the other hand, present virtually seamless fabrics. To be sure, these plays still offer internal sketches with external commentary, but here commentary and play-within are leading toward the same goal; as we have noted, the works of Trapwit and Fustian, like Medley's brief skits, are not so much the objects of satire as the agents of it. And the audience cannot mistake the satiric intent of these internal objects because they, unlike those found in *The Author's Farce*, have unmistakable political applications. That is to say, in *Pasquin* and *The Historical Register*—to recall the critical terminology of my earlier analysis—politics is the distancing device that prevents misinterpretation. The plays' exuberance derives from Fielding's knowledge that he is fully in control, that his motives cannot possibly be misinterpreted, because he has discovered a dramatic metaphor that yokes together all the potentially fissiparous elements of modernity, the quintessential link connecting all the pleasures of the town to their political source.

The political state of Walpole's England, then, is the tenor of Fielding's dramatic metaphor in his last plays; the theatrical representation of the pleasures of the town, with all the difficulties involved in that representation, is the vehicle. *The Historical Register* and *Eurydice Hiss'd* give special bite to the dramatic metaphor by particularizing the satire, by choosing sides. In *The Historical Register* Fielding mocks those who, like the first player and perhaps like the author of *Pasquin*, believe that satire is simply the repetition of general and hackneyed condemnations. In the first player's words,

"I would repeat in every page that courtiers are cheats and don't pay their debts, that lawyers are rogues, physicians blockheads, soldiers cowards, and ministers" (1 [13]). Just at the moment when he appears to hit a specific target, the first player draws back: "I'll only name 'em, that's enough to set the audience a-hooting" (ibid.). Like the writers of "simple" farces, a term Honestus uses in *Eurydice Hiss'd* (Appleton, ed., p. 68) to classify *Eurydice*, the first player is satisfied with an automatic response. A response of any kind, as Fielding well understood, is better than no response: it is preferable "to set the audience a-hooting" than a-sleeping. The playwright's first goal is to entertain his audience. As Medley observes with tongue in cheek, the "main design" of his "several plots"—"some pretty deep and some but shallow"—is "to divert the town and bring full houses" (1 [15]). But drama must also teach, must have a moral (ibid.). It is not enough to "extract" satirical tags from "above a dozen plays" (p. 13), as the first player admits; one must aim for specificity, one must select what is really important, what is historically meaningful. One must, in short, write a quintessential play like *The Historical Register*, though Medley is less than candid when he says, like Tacitus at the beginning of his *Annals*, that his "design is to ridicule the vicious and foolish customs of the age, and that in a fair manner, without fear, favor, or ill-nature" (p. 15). What distinguishes Medley's quintessential "design" from the first player's "humming deal of satire"—and from Fielding's previous plays—is its "favor," its ill-natured barbs at the ministry, its specific partisan applications. In Walpole's England, a "humming deal of satire" is not enough; the socially conscious dramatist can no longer play along with the general farce and "screen" the culprit;[13] he no longer has the easy alternative, the cowardly luxury, of writing *sine ira et studio*.

    This irruption of political reality into the playhouse is reflected in the odd title of Medley's new play, *The Historical Register*, a title made even more specific in Fielding's *Historical Register for the Year 1736*. Sourwit, as he tells Medley, is "a little staggered at the name of your piece. Doubtless, sir, you know the rules of writing, and I can't guess how you can bring the actions of a whole year into the circumference of four-and-twenty-hours" (p. 14). Like all carping critics in rehearsal plays, Sourwit is a devout Aristotelian and cannot imagine how a "whole year" can be compressed into that all-important dramatic "day"; of course, he fails to take into account that he has never seen a twenty-four-hour play, that the quintessence of the dramatist's art is selection. Medley now reminds him of this curious property of the dramatist's mirror. His new play, he points out, is not like "vulgar" newspapers, often "filled . . . with trash for lack of news" (p. 15). Its journalistic title, in this respect, has misled the literal-minded critic. Instead, his "piece," as Sourwit calls it, selects or "extracts," from the larger register of historical events, what is truly significant; hence, it can depict, "in half an hour," every single action that captures the quintessence of the year. In fact, Medley's model is so successful that, with only a few strokes of his satiric brush, in his scene on taxation he can portray ("comprise" is Medley's word) "the full account of the whole history of Europe" (p. 21). But Medley's dramatic allegory, its artistic transformations notwithstanding, is firmly grounded in history. The allegorical scenes of *The Historical Register* may have wider applications to—in Hume's oft-quoted phrase—the constant and universal principles of human nature. But their most important connection is to specific events in a specific place (England) during a specific year (1736).

One of the most newsworthy events of the year, as the town well knew, had occurred not in the turbulent world of politics, where all eyes (and ears) had been riveted in fascination and ever-mounting anxiety, but in the lesser, though equally volatile, world of the theater. On the night of 19 February 1737, *Eurydice*, Fielding's one-act afterpiece to Addison's *Cato*, had been damned at Drury Lane, drowned in a deafening din of hisses, whistles, and catcalls, by a mob of unruly footmen. This disastrous event had apparently occurred too late in the calendar year—then reckoned to run until March—to be included in the dramatic allegory of *The Historical Register for the Year 1736* when the play opened on 21 March 1737.[14] On 13 April, however, Fielding corrected this omission and added to his already popular play what was in effect a new act, *Eurydice Hiss'd or A Word to the Wise*. In this brief sketch Fielding extended his dramatic allegory to its boldest application yet, as the playwright-within of Spatter's "tragedy," the "very Great Man" Pillage (p. 56), becomes not only the symbol of the corrupt man of the theater who will balk at nothing to make a profit—Fielding's most honest self-portrait—but also the dramatic counterpart of the Great Man of English politics, Sir Robert Walpole, who had recently failed in what was widely regarded as one of his crudest attempts on the liberties of the king's long-suffering subjects. Just as Fielding and his ill-fated *Eurydice* had been hooted off the stage at Drury Lane, so had Walpole and his ministers been soundly humiliated, both in the press and in Parliament, for trying to act out their little public farce known as the Excise Bill. As the earl of Egmont noted in his diary, the parallels between stage and state could not be mistaken: "To the Haymarket playhouse where a farce was acted called *Eurydice First* [*sic*] an allegory on the loss of the Excise Bill. The whole was a satire on Sir Robert Walpole, and I observed that when any strong passages fell, the Prince [Frederick] who was there, clapped, especially when in favor of liberty." [15]

But, as he would continue to do until 1742, Sir Robert had the last laugh. On 21 June 1737 the Licensing Act received the royal assent, and three days later, on 24 June, the Little Theatre in the Haymarket closed its doors. Like the "actor standing in the wings laugh[ing] loudly" in *The Historical Register*, Sir Robert, his nose tweaked once too often by the Opposition wits, had been plotting "behind the scenes" (p. 46). As the curtain fell for the last time on that gloomy summer's evening at Mr. Fielding's "scandal-shop," the Great Man stepped forward to speak his triumphant epilogue, while the Great Mogul, no match for his allegorical double, fled backstage, followed by his "Company of Comedians," to pick up the pieces of his shattered satiric mirror. That satiric mirror, wondrously reconstituted, would, like the ghost of Queen Common-Sense, continue to haunt the prime minister—in the *Champion*, in *Jonathan Wild*—but it would never again recapture its original effulgence, the bright, living images of flesh and blood it projected onto the London stage during the glorious final days of Fielding's dramatic career. [16]

138

NOTES

INDEX

Notes

Preface

1. Robert D. Hume, "Henry Fielding and Politics at the Little Haymarket, 1728–1737," in John M. Wallace, ed., *The Golden & the Brazen World: Papers in Literature and History, 1650–1800* (Berkeley and Los Angeles: Univ. of California Press, 1985), p. 79.

2. Jean Ducrocq, *Le théâtre de Fielding, 1728–1737, et ses prolongements dans l'oeuvre romanesque* (Dijon, 1975).

3. Pat Rogers, *Henry Fielding: A Biography* (New York: Charles Scribner's Sons, 1979), p. 233.

4. See, for example, Anthony J. Hassall, "The Authorial Dimension in the Plays of Henry Fielding," *Komos* 1 (1967): 4–18; J. Paul Hunter, *Occasional Form: Henry Fielding and the Chains of Circumstance* (Baltimore: Johns Hopkins Univ. Press, 1975), pp. 23–74; and Marsha Kinder, "Henry Fielding's Dramatic Experimentations: A Preface to His Fiction," Ph.D. Diss., University of California, Los Angeles, 1967.

5. Robert D. Hume, *Henry Fielding and the London Theatre, 1728–1737* (Oxford: Clarendon Press, 1988).

6. Simon Varey, *The Clark Newsletter* (Spring 1985), p. 6.

7. For an account of theatrical affairs in London during this period, see Arthur H. Scouten's introduction to *The London Stage, 1660–1800*, Part 3: *1729–1747* (Carbondale: Southern Illinois Univ. Press, 1961), 1:xix-clxxxviii; and Robert D. Hume, "The London Theatre from *The Beggar's Opera* to the Licensing Act," in Hume, *The Rakish Stage: Studies in English Drama, 1660–1800* (Carbondale: Southern Illinois Univ. Press, 1983), pp. 270–311.

Introduction

1. Preface to the *First Volume of Plays: Pleasant and Unpleasant* (1906), reprinted in *Complete Plays with Prefaces* (New York: Dodd, Mead, 1963), 3:xvi.

2. C. B. Woods, Introduction to Woods, ed., *The Author's Farce* (Lincoln: Univ. of Nebraska Press, 1966), p. xii.

3. *An Apology for the Life of Mr. Colley Cibber, Comedian* (London, 1740), p. 164.

4. Thus Martin C. Battestin, in his introduction to *Tom Jones*, observes that Fielding's "years as a playwright were important primarily for what they meant to the novels: the theatre sharpened Fielding's ear for comic dialogue and perfected that sense of form, of significant design, which is one of his chief contributions to the art of fiction" (Fredson Bowers, ed., *The History of Tom Jones: A Foundling* [Middletown, Conn.: Wesleyan Univ. Press, 1975], p. xvii). All citations are to this edition.

5. I am not denying the value of cross-genre studies. Indeed, I think that our difficulties in determining the generic interrelations between the drama and the novel derive from our imperfect understanding of the issues involved. We have based our hypotheses on faulty premises. In the case of early eighteenth-century drama, we have moved too quickly toward the novel, toward the apparent *telos*, without pausing to consider what was actually happening in the theater. For an excellent exposition of the complexities of the subject—complexities students of early eighteenth-century drama have managed, for the most part, to ignore—see Ralph Cohen, "On the Interrelations of Eighteenth-Century Literary Forms," in Phillip Harth, ed., *New Approaches to Eighteenth-Century Literature* (New York: Columbia Univ. Press, 1974), pp. 33–78.

6. For an analysis of the changes in English society that gave rise to changes in the conception of comedy, especially of dramatic comedy, see John Loftis, *Comedy and Society from Congreve to Fielding* (Stanford: Stanford Univ. Press, 1959). On the changes in taste and attitude of London theater audiences from Dryden to Sheridan, see Leo Hughes, *The Drama's Patrons: A Study of the Eighteenth-Century London Audience* (Austin: Univ. of Texas Press, 1971). Fielding deeply respected the work of the author of *The London Merchant* (1731) and, as manager of the Little Haymarket, staged Lillo's *Fatal Curiosity* (1736), for which he wrote the prologue.

7. For example, a recent study of eighteenth-century drama, told from the perspective of regular forms and the novel, manages to reach its conclusions without mentioning John Gay once. Given that *The Beggar's Opera* was the most popular and influential play of the eighteenth century, I find this a curious omission. Fielding's irregular drama is referred to only in passing, in a section about the relative failure of his regular plays. See Laura Brown, *English Dramatic Form, 1660–1760: An Essay in Generic History* (New Haven: Yale Univ. Press, 1981).

8. *The Author's Farce*, ed. Woods, p. 16.

9. In "Henry Fielding and Politics at the Little Haymarket." Robert D. Hume observes that Fielding's return to the Haymarket with *Don Quixote in England* "had nothing to do with politics" (p. 93). I agree with Hume that the *staging* of the play need not be read in political terms; however, the *dedication*, to one of the leaders of the Opposition, must be understood as an overt political move. See also Hume, *Henry Fielding and the London Theatre*, pp. 183–84.

CHAPTER I
A Bow to the Tradition:
Love in Several Masques and *The Temple Beau*

1. Emmett L. Avery, ed., *The London Stage, 1600–1800*, Part 2: 1700–1729 (Carbondale: Southern Illinois Univ. Press, 1960), pp. 959–60.

2. W. E. Henley, ed., *The Works of Henry Fielding, Esq.* (New York: Croscup & Sterling, 1902), 8:9. Further references to this play appear within the text and will indicate act, scene, and page number in Henley. Until the publication of the Wesleyan edition of the plays, now two decades overdue, the critic must make do with Henley's edition. Although I have read all the plays in their original London editions, I draw all my citations from Henley unless otherwise indicated.

3. In *Henry Fielding and the London Theatre*, after asserting that the hypothesis "that Lady Mary exercised significant influence in getting the piece staged is quite unlikely," Hume goes on to grant that she "might have introduced Fielding to one of the managers (if she knew any of them), or to someone who could do so" (pp. 29–30).

4. *The Laureat: or, The Right Side of Colley Cibber, Esq.* (London, 1740), pp. 66–67.

5. Edward Niles Hooker, ed., *The Critical Works of John Dennis* (Baltimore: Johns Hopkins Press, 1943), 2:278–79. For a similar assessment seven years later, see *A Proposal for the better regulation of the stage* (London, 1732), esp. pp. 8, 21–22. James Ralph, in *The Case of our Present Theatrical Disputes, Fairly Stated* (London, 1743), offers a rare dissenting view: "When the Triumvirate governed in *Drury-Lane*, the Playhouse was the best regulated State in Europe" (p. 27). But Ralph's praise must be understood in the context of the dramatic controversy in which he was then engaged; six years after the Licensing Act of 1737, Ralph needs to establish that there was a time when theatrical matters were admirably run by theater people, without any government interference.

6. *Critical Works of Dennis*, ed. Hooker, 2:277.

7. Ibid., p. 275.

8. Ibid.

9. Ibid., p. 385.

10. Preface to *Plutus* (London, 1742), p. xi. In *Tom Jones* (12.5) Tom and Partridge attend a Puppet show reenacting "the fine and serious Part of the *Provok'd Husband;* and it was indeed a very grave and solemn Entertainment, without any low Wit or Humour, or Jests; or . . . without any thing which could provoke a Laugh" (p. 638). Although "the Audience were all highly pleased," Tom believes that "by leaving out [Master *Punch*] and his merry Wife *Joan*," the "improving" puppet-master has "spoiled [his] Puppet-show" (pp. 638–39). In short, both the puppet master and Cibber, by attempting to improve, have spoiled their respective comic traditions.

11. Robert D. Hume, *The Development of English Drama in the Late Seventeenth Century* (Oxford: Clarendon Press, 1976), pp. 411–15.

12. This passage, together with an excerpt from Thomas Davies's *Dramatic Miscellanies* (1784) describing the play's opening night, is quoted in *The London Stage*, Part 2, 2:954.

13. *Tom Jones*, p. 640.

14. Colley Cibber, *The Provok'd Husband: or, A Journey to London* (London, 1728), p. 1.

15. "Prologue Spoken by Mr. Garrick, at the Opening of the Theatre in Drury-Lane 1747," ll. 53–54, in Bertrand H. Bronson, ed., *Samuel Johnson: Rasselas, Poems, and Selected Prose* (San Francisco: Rinehart, 1952), p. 51.

16. Cibber, *Apology*, p. 68.

17. Cibber, To the Reader of *The Provok'd Husband*, p. 2.

18. Although most of Cibber's verbal blunders were corrected in the play's second edition, references to them abound, sometimes in rather odd contexts. For instance, Cibber's awkward commendation of Mrs. Oldfield's acting ("Here [she] *Out-did* her usual *Out-doing*") shows up thus in Henry Carey's *Chrononhotonthologos* (1734), as Aldiborontiphoscophornio replies to the King's "What ails the Queen?": "A sudden *Diarrhoea's* rapid Force, / So stimulates the Peristaltic Motion, / That she by far out-does her late Out-doing / And all conclude her Royal Life in Danger" (*The Dramatick Works of Henry Carey* [London, 1743], p. 166).

19. L. P. Goggin remarks Fielding's inability to unify his plots in his early plays, an inability he gradually overcame ("Development of Techniques in Fielding's Comedies," *PMLA* 67 [1952]: 769–81). For his comments on *Love in Several Masques*, see p. 775. In his eagerness to trace

a development, Goggin fails to note why certain techniques function the way they do in individual plays. He divorces these techniques from their context, from those thematic purposes they are meant to implement. This is a serious flaw in what is otherwise a most important contribution to our understanding of Fielding's dramatic method. See also Winfield H. Rogers, "Fielding's Early Aesthetic and Technique," *Studies in Philology* 40 (1943): 529–51.

20. Hume, *Fielding and the London Theatre*, p. 30.

21. See *Tom Jones*, 7.1: "A Comparison between the World and the Stage." Cf. Irvin Ehrenpreis, *Fielding: Tom Jones* (London: Edward Arnold, 1964), p. 40: "The stage devices of *Tom Jones* remind one endlessly that art reveals the truth through seeming, while life misleads us through artfulness."

22. For this aspect of Fielding's last novel, see Martin C. Battestin, "The Problem of *Amelia*: Hume, Barrow, and the Conversion of Captain Booth," *English Literary History* 41 (1974): 613–48.

23. Henry K. Miller, ed., *Miscellanies* (1743), Volume One (Oxford: Oxford University Press, 1972), p. 155. For an analysis of Fielding's use of the masquerade in *Amelia*, see Terry Castle, *Masquerade and Civilization: The Carnivalesque in Eighteenth-Century English Culture and Fiction* (Stanford: Stanford Univ. Press, 1986), pp. 177–252.

24. *The London Stage*, Part 3, 1:34–35. *The Temple Beau* was probably the third or fourth play Fielding wrote. *Don Quixote in England*, acted in 1734, he began to compose at Leyden, and *The Wedding Day*, acted in 1742, he refers to as "the third Dramatic Performance I ever attempted" in the preface to the *Miscellanies*, ed., Miller, pp. 4–5. On the order of composition of these plays, see Hume, *Fielding and the London Theatre*, pp. 44–46.

25. *The London Stage*, Part 3, 1:xxi. On "The Advent of Goodman's Fields," see Hume, *Fielding and the London Theatre*, pp. 39–44.

26. Henley, 8:103. In a brief but perceptive chapter on the plays in *The World Upside-Down: Comedy from Jonson to Fielding* (Oxford: Oxford Univ. Press, 1970), Ian Donaldson has argued that Fielding is a comic, not a satiric, dramatist. I agree with Donaldson that Fielding believed that matters, at least those matters dealt with in the supremely artificial medium of comedy, will turn out right, but this comic view of life does not preclude a satiric stance. Fielding's satire in most of his plays is Horatian: he endeavors "to laugh Mankind out of their favourite Follies and Vices" (dedication to *Tom Jones*, p. 8). This type of benevolent satire is not incompatible with a comic vision.

27. Cf. Harriet's speech in *The Miser* (3.8): "In my opinion, the coquette, who sacrifices the ease and reputation of as many as she is able to

an ill-natured vanity, is a more odious, I am sure she is a more pernicious creature, than the wretch whom fondness betrays to make her lover happy at the expense of her own reputation" (Henley, 10 [226]).

CHAPTER 2

The Apprentice Finds His Voice:
The Author's Farce (1730)

1. For further details about the stage and publication history of *The Author's Farce*, see Woods's introduction to his edition. Citations to the play will be from this edition.

2. See George Winchester Stone, Jr., "The Making of the Repertory," in Robert D. Hume, ed., *The London Theatre World, 1660–1800* (Carbondale: Southern Illinois Univ. Press, 1980), pp. 181–209. On Shakespeare's increasing popularity, see Charles B. Hogan, *Shakespeare in the Theatre, 1701–1800: London, 1701–1750* (Oxford: Clarendon Press, 1952) and Allardyce Nicoll, *A History of Early Eighteenth Century Drama, 1700–1750* (Cambridge: Cambridge Univ. Press, 1925), esp. pp. 66–70.

3. On this improvement see Hume, *Fielding and the London Theatre*, pp. 35–39.

4. *Tumble-Down Dick or Phaeton in the Suds* (1736), "To Mr. John Lun, Vulgarly called Esquire," in Henley, 12:7; John Rich appears on stage as Mr. Machine, to reassure Fustian that his Ovidian entertainment is "serious" (p. 14).

5. Woods, ed., *The Author's Farce*, Introduction, p. xv.

6. Cross, *The History of Henry Fielding* (New Haven: Yale Univ. Press, 1918), 1:80.

7. See Miller, ed., *Miscellanies*, pp. 4–8.

8. On the subject of contemporary entertainments, see the following articles by Emmett L. Avery: "Dancing and Pantomime on the English Stage, 1700–1737," *Studies in Philology* 21 (1934): 417–52; "Vaudeville on the London Stage, 1700–1737," *Research Studies of the State College of Washington* 5 (1937): 65–77; "Foreign Performers in the London Theatres in the Early Eighteenth Century," *Philological Quarterly* 16 (1937): 105–23; and "The Defense and Criticism of Pantomimic Entertainments in the Eighteenth Century," *English Literary History* 5 (1938): 127–45. See also K. G. Ruttkay, "The Critical Reception of Italian Opera in England in the Early Eighteenth Century," *Studies in English and American Philology* 1 (1971): 93–169. That operas, pantomimes, dances, and the like were deplored for their intellectual vacuity, for their emphasis on

sound and movement to the detriment of sense, by men of various dramatic tastes and prejudices, should not obscure the crucial fact that they *were* entertaining, and, because their popular appeal could not be ignored, they forced contemporary dramatists to transform their works to accommodate them; thus, they made an enormous contribution to the creation and revitalization of dramatic forms in the early eighteenth-century.

9. In the 1734 version of *The Author's Farce*, however, the play is explicitly labeled a tragedy, as Fielding throws into even sharper relief the distinctions among the various modes of mimesis which *The Author's Farce*, as a whole, examines: the prose of the frame, the blank verse of Luckless's fragment, the occasional musical interludes, and the emblematic, "non-representational" puppet show.

10. *The Plays of John Gay* (London: Abbey Classics, 1923), 1:34. For a reading of this play, see Peter E. Lewis, "Gay's Burlesque Method in *The What D'Ye Call It*," *Durham University Journal* 29 (1967): 13–25.

11. Wilkes, *A General View of the Stage* (London, 1759), pp. 60–61.

12. See Nahum Tate's 1693 preface to his *A Duke and No Duke* (1684). For this brief excursus on farce, I have drawn mainly on Leo Hughes, *A Century of English Farce* (Princeton: Princeton Univ. Press, 1956), esp. ch. 1.

13. Henley, 8:267, ll. 2, 4, 5–9. This prologue was originally spoken by Theophilus Cibber.

14. A recent article has stressed the importance of Molière's histrionic training and staging procedures in interpreting his plays. See Roger W. Herzel, "'Much Depends on the Acting': The Original Cast of *Le Misanthrope*," *PMLA* 95 (1980): 348–66. For Molière's debt to the Italians, see Philip A. Wadsworth, *Molière and the Italian Theatrical Tradition* (N.p.: French Literature Publications Co., 1977).

15. *Tom Jones*, p. 686. For further references to Molière in Fielding's works, see Battestin's note to this passage.

16. For the possible classical source of Bookweight's distinction between acting and reading plays, see Aristotle, *On Poetry and Style*, trans., G. M. A. Grube (New York: Bobbs-Merrill, 1958), p. 15: "A tragedy can achieve its effect apart from the performance and the actors. Indeed, spectacular effects belong to the craft of the property man rather than to that of the poet." Cf. *A Proposal for the better regulation of the stage*, p. 25: "A good Player is as necessary to the Dramatick Writer as good Language, and Energy of Expression; and, on the other hand, a Player without the Writer is a Page of Blank-Paper, only a Vehicle to Thought, and of no Importance till animated with the Soul, and Genius of Poetry."

17. Miller, ed., *Miscellanies*, p. 5.

18. *Harlequin-Horace* (4th ed., 1741), note to line 120.

19. For an analysis of this mock anagnorisis, see Valerie C. Rudolph, "People and Puppets: Fielding's Burlesque on the 'Recognition Scene' in *The Author's Farce*," *Papers on Language and Literature* 11 (1975): 31–38.

20. See, for example, "Stap my breath!" (p. 46), the boast of linguistic innovation, "Stap my vitals!" and "one bone" (p. 55), the two references to *Love in a Riddle* (pp. 45, 68), and the justly celebrated "Paraphonalia" from the address "To the Reader" of *The Provok'd Husband* (p. 68). For the sources of these allusions in Cibber's works, see Woods's notes to these passages.

21. For further historical identifications, see Woods's notes and Appendix B. I have not repeated this material here because it is already available elsewhere and I have little to add to what Woods and others have discovered. For the possible political significance of these contemporary references, see Sheridan Baker, "Political Allusion in Fielding's *Author's Farce, Mock Doctor,* and *Tumble-Down Dick*," *PMLA* 77 (1962): 221–31. I concur with Woods's observation, *contra* Baker, that "there seems to be little political satire in the 1730 text," but that "there is nothing far-fetched about his [Baker's] seeing political implications in passages Fielding added in 1734" (p. xv, n. 4). See also Bertrand A. Goldgar, *Walpole and the Wits: The Relations of Politics to Literature, 1722–1742* (Lincoln: Univ. of Nebraska Press, 1976), pp. 102–4; Hume, *Fielding and the London Theatre*, p. 66; and Jean B. Kern, *Dramatic Satire in the Age of Walpole, 1720–1750* (Ames: Iowa State Univ. Press, 1976).

22. Marjorie Williams, ed., *The Letters of William Shenstone* (Oxford: Oxford Univ. Press, 1939), p. 48, letter dated May 1742.

23. See Hassall, "The Authorial Dimension in the Plays of Henry Fielding"; Hunter, *Occasional Form;* and C. J. Rawson, "Some Considerations on Authorial Intrusion in Fielding's Novels and Plays," *Durham University Journal* 33 (1971): 32–44.

24. See Hassall, "Fielding's Puppet Image," *Philological Quarterly* 53 (1974): 71–83.

25. Hunter, *Occasional Form*, p. 69.

26. See Ira Konigsberg, *Samuel Richardson and the Dramatic Novel* (Lexington: Univ. of Kentucky Press, 1968) and Mark Kinkead-Weekes, *Samuel Richardson: Dramatic Novelist* (Ithaca, N.Y.: Cornell Univ. Press, 1973). Richardson, however, saw the limits of the purely representational for a moral writer. His footnotes and index to *Clarissa*, both added after the "dramatic" first edition was misinterpreted by readers who, like Aaron Hill and Lady Bradshaigh, Richardson felt should have known better, are

only the most prominent devices by which he tried to guide his reader's responses. For examples of Richardson's more subtle authorial manipulation, see William Beatty Warner, *Reading Clarissa: The Struggles of Interpretation* (New Haven: Yale Univ. Press, 1979).

27. Ian Watt's *The Rise of the Novel: Studies in Defoe, Richardson, and Fielding* (Berkeley and Los Angeles: Univ. of California Press, 1957) is the best exponent of this view. Because Watt's main criterion for the novel is realism, and realism as he defines it excludes an authorial presence, he cannot consider Fielding a true novelist. For different approaches to the subject, see Wayne C. Booth, *The Rhetoric of Fiction* (Chicago: Univ. of Chicago Press, 1961) and Robert Scholes and Robert Kellogg, *The Nature of Narrative* (Oxford: Oxford Univ. Press, 1966).

28. Rawson, "Authorial Intrusion," p. 35.

29. For a survey of the English rehearsal play, see Dane Farnsworth Smith's complementary studies, *Plays about the Theatre in England from "The Rehearsal" in 1671 to the Licensing Act of 1737* (Oxford: Oxford Univ. Press, 1936) and *The Critics in the Audience of the London Theatres from Buckingham to Sheridan: A Study of Neoclassicism in the Playhouse, 1671–1779* (Albuquerque: Univ. of New Mexico Press, 1953).

30. Aristotle, *On Poetry and Style*, pp. 3–15 passim. Tragedy, for Aristotle, was the normative dramatic form. Later theorists, especially in France, in the seventeenth and eighteenth centuries, would interpret the *Poetics* as a prescriptive treatise and apply its rules to both tragedy and comedy. I am aware that my discussion of mimesis and catharsis simplifies a most complex issue; catharsis, in particular, is a most troublesome term. Its meaning in the *Poetics* is nebulous at best; reference to other appearances in Aristotle's works—most notably in the *Politics*—can suggest possible medical and educational contexts for the word but little by way of a precise definition. For discussions of these issues, see L. P. Golden, "Mimesis and Catharsis," *Classical Philology* 64 (1969): 45–53; and Martha C. Nussbaum, *The Fragility of Goodness: Luck and Ethics in Greek Tragedy and Philosophy* (Cambridge: Cambridge Univ. Press, 1986), pp. 388–91. The literature on the subject is, of course, vast; an annotated bibliography of the most prominent interpretations of catharsis appears in Stephen Halliwell, *Aristotle's Poetics* (Chapel Hill: Univ. of North Carolina Press, 1986), Appendix 5, pp. 350–56.

31. That dramatic performances can have powerful emotional effects on their audiences is illustrated in the story, well-circulated in antiquity, of women frightened into giving premature birth during a production of Aeschylus' *Eumenides*. For Brecht's concept of alienation (*Verfremdung*), see *Gesammelte Werke*, 21 vols. (Frankfurt: Suhrkamp Ver-

lag, 1967), 17:1008–9. For discussions of Brecht's epic theatre, see Keith A. Dickson, "Brecht: An Aristotelian *malgré lui*," *Modern Drama* 11 (1968): 111–21; "Of Masks and Men: An Aspect of Brecht's Theatrical Technique," *New German Studies* 1 (1973): 1–14; and, by the same author, *Towards Utopia: A Study of Brecht* (Oxford: Oxford Univ. Press, 1978), esp. pp. 228 ff.; Martin Esslin, *Bertolt Brecht* (New York: Columbia Univ. Press, 1969), esp. entries under "intellectual" in index; and W. A. J. Steer, "Brecht's Epic Theatre: Theory and Practice," *Modern Language Review* 62 (1968): 636–49.

32. For the notion of imitation as revenge, see René Girard, *La Violence et le Sacré* (Paris: Grasset et Fasquelle, 1972), esp. ch. 6, "Du Désir Mimétique au Double Monstrueux," pp. 201–34.

33. Hassall, "Fielding's Puppet Image," p. 76. For Fielding's later role as master of a puppet show, see Martin C. Battestin, "Fielding and 'Master Punch' in Panton Street," *Philological Quarterly* 45 (1966): 191–208. For a general survey and study of puppet shows in England, see George Speaight, *The History of the English Puppet Theatre* (London: G. G. Harrap, 1955).

34. James Boswell, *Life of Johnson* (Oxford: Oxford Univ. Press, 1970), p. 731 (entry for Friday, 5 April 1776).

CHAPTER 3

The Life and Critical Opinions of
H. Scriblerus Secundus:
Tom Thumb and *The Tragedy of Tragedies*

1. For the stage history of *Tom Thumb* and *The Tragedy of Tragedies*, see the pertinent entries in *The London Stage*, Part 3, vol. 1, and the introductions to the two modern editions of the plays by J. T. Hillhouse (New Haven: Yale Univ. Press, 1918) and L. J. Morrissey (Berkeley and Los Angeles: Univ. of California Press, 1970). All quotations from *Tom Thumb* and *The Tragedy of Tragedies* are from Morrissey's edition; citations appear in text.

2. Woods, ed., *The Author's Farce*, p. 53.

3. D. E. L. Crane, ed., *The Rehearsal* (Durham, England: Univ. of Durham Press, 1976), pp. 16, 18.

4. For an account of Fielding's debt to Buckingham's play, see Samuel L. Macey, "Fielding's *Tom Thumb* as the Heir to Buckingham's *Rehearsal*," *Texas Studies in Literature and Language* 10 (1968): 405–14.

5. See the prologue to *Tom Thumb*, p. 20. Cf. the prologue to *The Author's Farce* and Luckless's comments to the player at the beginning of his puppet show, pp. 39–41. In *Harlequin-Horace* (ll. 174–75, and footnote), James Miller comments on the generic mixtures of "our modern Dramatick Writers": "Their Comedies have such very *Sad* Scenes in them, that they seldom fail to draw Tears from the tender and compassionate Part of the Audience; whilst on the contrary their Tragedies are so pleasant and diverting, that the Spectators can't refrain from frequently bursting into a Laugh."

6. Preface to *Tom Thumb*, p. 18. Cf. Addison's observations on the improprieties of "Tragi-Comedy" in *The Spectator*, no. 40 (16 April 1711), ed. Donald F. Bond (Oxford: Clarendon Press, 1965), 1:170: "The Tragi-Comedy, which is the Product of the *English* Theatre, is one of the most monstrous Inventions that ever enter'd into a Poet's Thoughts. An Author might as well think of weaving the Adventures of *Aeneas* and *Hudibras* into one Poem, as of writing such a motly Piece of Mirth and Sorrow."

7. J. Hillis Miller, "Stevens' Rock and Criticism as Cure, II," *Georgia Review* 30 (1976): 341.

8. See, for example, Lord Dapper's confusion of real and stage auctions in *The Historical Register for the Year 1736*, ed. William W. Appleton (Lincoln: Univ. of Nebraska Press, 1967), p. 34: "Egad, you took me in, Mr. Medley. I could not help bidding for it."

9. Preface to *Tom Thumb*, p. 17. In *The Analysis of Beauty*, ed. Joseph Burke (Oxford: Oxford Univ. Press, 1955), William Hogarth observes that "when improper, or *incompatible* excesses meet, they always excite laughter" (p. 48). In a rejected passage (British Library, Egmont Ms. 3015, f. 65b), Hogarth applies this principle to Fielding's play: "So Tom Thumb in the Tragedy of Tragedys doth not a little contribute to the humour of that piece [in which example] it is the inconsistancys and extravagant incompatibleness, that work drollery." This passage is cited in Burke's edition, p. 186.

10. Hunter, *Occasional Form*, p. 23. Hunter deals with the deeper resonances of the size metaphor on pp. 38–40.

11. Bond, ed., *The Spectator*, no. 42 (18 April 1711), 1:178. See numbers 39, 40, and 44 for Addison's additional comments on the many shortcomings of heroic tragedy, from its stultifying rhymes (39) and "ranting" diction (40) to its mechanical reliance on stage "artifices" to "fill the Minds of an Audience with Terrour" (44).

12. Both versions of the play burgeon with innuendos about the little man's sexual inadequacy. See, for example, p. 31, and Epilogue (*Tom*

Thumb); and pp. 51, 67, 70, and 71 (*The Tragedy of Tragedies*). This last instance leads into Grizzle's famous panegyric on Huncamunca's globelike breasts (pp. 71–72).

13. *Tom Thumb*, p. 27. In *The Tragedy of Tragedies*, the enraptured Doodle can account for the hero's greatness only by venturing that he must be of divine stock: "Some God . . . stept into the Place / Of Gaffer *Thumb*, and more than half begot, / This mighty *Tom*" (p. 51).

14. In a sadly neglected article published six decades ago, Helen Sard Hughes suggests that Fielding may have found the inspiration for choosing a native tragic hero in *The Touch-Stone*, a compendium of "the Reigning Diversions of the Town" written by his friend and sometime collaborator, James Ralph. Hughes supports her thesis with passages from Ralph which anticipate the language and views of Fielding's prefaces to *Tom Thumb* and *The Tragedy of Tragedies;* her argument is less persuasive in regard to *The Author's Farce*. See "Fielding's Indebtedness to James Ralph," *Modern Philology* 20 (1922): 19–34. In his introduction to the plays (cited in n. 1, above, pp. 6–9), J. T. Hillhouse suggests William Wagstaffe's *A Comment upon the History of Tom Thumb* (1711), a mock elaboration of Addison's advice to British tragedians, as another plausible source for Fielding's play.

15. See Scriblerus's first footnote to *The Tragedy of Tragedies*, p. 49.

16. The anecdote is reported by Mrs. Pilkington in the third volume of her memoirs (London, 1754, p. 155; cited by Hillhouse, p. 150). In *Harlequin-Horace*, James Miller recalls the "Surprize" given by Tom Thumb, "from the *Cow's Maw*, thrown up again alive" (ll. 534–35). In a footnote added to the fourth edition of the poem in 1741, Miller records that "this Piece of Advice has been literally follow'd since the first Publication of this Poem; The Directors of the several Theatres having reviv'd the Farce of *Tom Thumb*, with an additional Scene of this Marvellous *Incident*, wherein the Cow is said to have perform'd her Part beyond Expectation, and disgorg'd her little Inhabitant in full Health and Vigour, and in a Manner entirely Satisfactory to the transported Beholders. A sufficient Encouragement, we presume, to every Bard to persevere in all the Rules laid down in our Work."

17. Most of Scriblerus's volleys derive from his eponymous ancestor's rules for achieving the "profound" in Pope's *Peri Bathous: Or, The Art of Sinking in Poetry*, especially from those rules, recorded in the tenth and eleventh chapters, which deal with the "variegating, confounding . . . reversing . . . Magnifying and diminishing" of "Tropes and Figures." For a detailed study of Fielding's concern with the corruption of language, see

Glenn W. Hatfield, *Henry Fielding and the Language of Irony* (Chicago: Univ. of Chicago Press, 1968). Like other scholars, Hatfield stresses the similarities between Fielding's views on the subject and those found in the third book of Locke's *Essay concerning Human Understanding* (1690; 4th ed., extensively revised, 1700).

18. F. N. Robinson, ed., *The Works of Geoffrey Chaucer* (New York: Houghton Mifflin, 1957), p. 167.

19. See, for example, the *Grub-Street Journal* (7 May, 11 June, 17 December 1730; 18 November 1731). Since Walpole was reputed to have attended *Tom Thumb* three times, *Fog's Weekly Journal* (1 August 1730) refers to the minister's patronage of it and *Hurlothrumbo* as proof of his lack of taste and encouragement of bad art, a sentiment echoed three weeks later by the *Craftsman* (22 August 1730). If Fielding's work had antiministerial overtones, as several critics have suggested, Walpole was apparently deaf to them. But if the play contained no overt political allusions, the attacks on it were decidedly partisan. The Opposition journals chose to ignore the satiric purpose of Fielding's piece in order to use it as a tool against Walpole's alleged gaucheries in government as well as in aesthetics. On the political import of *Tom Thumb* and *The Tragedy of Tragedies*, see L. J. Morrissey, "Fielding's First Political Satire," *Anglia* 90 (1972): 325–48, and his introduction and notes to the plays (cited in n. 1, above), esp. pp. 4–6, 112, 115. Bertrand A. Goldgar offers a convincing rejoinder to this position in *Walpole and the Wits*, pp. 104–6; Goldgar's view is corroborated by Hume, *Fielding and the London Theatre*, pp. 89–91.

20. For Scriblerus's praise of these "little Aphorisms, which verbal Tradition hath delivered down to us, under the Title of Proverbs," see *The Tragedy of Tragedies*, p. 82.

21. Bertrand A. Goldgar, ed., *Literary Criticism of Alexander Pope* (Lincoln: Univ. of Nebraska Press, 1965), p. 65.

22. The reference is to lines 271–76, in which Jove weighs the "lots" of Hector and Achilles to determine the fated outcome of their duel on the Trojan plain: "Jove lifts the golden Balances, that show / The Fates of mortal Men, and things below: / Here each contending Hero's Lot he tries, / And weighs, with equal Hand, their Destinies. / Low sinks the Scale surcharg'd with Hector's Fate; / Heavy with Death it sinks, and Hell receives the Weight" (Reuben Brower and William H. Bond, eds., *The Iliad of Homer*, trans. Alexander Pope [New York: Collier, 1965], p. 497). H. Scriblerus Secundus cites two other "Pair[s] of Scales," from Dryden's *King Arthur* and *Don Sebastian* (*The Tragedy of Tragedies*, p. 63).

23. Hillhouse, pp. 149–50. The first edition of *Amelia* featured a

similarly redundant chapter (5.2) "Containing a Brace of Doctors, and much physical Matter." The chapter, deleted in later editions, ends with Fielding's recognition that "some Readers will perhaps think this whole Chapter might have been omitted; but though it contains no great Matter of Amusement, it may at least serve to inform Posterity concerning the present State of Physic." As always, Fielding is concerned with what Parson Adams, speaking of Homer's *Iliad*, calls "*Harmotton*" (3.2), a term which Martin C. Battestin, in *The Moral Basis of Fielding's Art: A Study of Joseph Andrews* (Middletown, Conn.: Wesleyan Univ. Press, 1959), glosses as "the correlation of structure and meaning" and cites to answer "those who are too ready to quarrel with Fielding for his ignorance of our post-Coleridgean shibboleth of organic unity" (p. 87). Battestin reprints the deleted chapter in Appendix II, pp. 540–42, of his edition of *Amelia* (Middletown, Conn.: Wesleyan Univ. Press, 1983).

24. Fielding added the initial of his name to that of Scriblerus Secundus only in *The Tragedy of Tragedies;* the author of *The Grub-Street Opera* is Scriblerus Secundus.

25. *The Tragedy of Tragedies*, pp. 80–81. This is Huncamunca's more "ample" version of her mother's "Scales." Unlike the queen, she refuses to choose.

26. Ibid., p. 82. This is the "little Aphorism" that so pleases Scriblerus (see note 20 above). For another instance of the conflict between love and honor rendered in equally bathetic and graphic terms, see King Volscius's predicament with his boots in *The Rehearsal*, p. 39.

27. Preface to *The Tragedy of Tragedies*, p. 42. For a selection of the most famous attacks on Fielding's play, see note 19 above and Hillhouse, pp. 12–23.

28. *The Letter Writers*, in Henley, 9:163.

29. Prologue to *The Modern Husband*, in Henley, 10:9.

30. In choosing the generic title for his expanded play, Fielding might have had in mind Bayes's words to Johnson and Smith in *The Rehearsal*, p. 49: "Now, Sirs I'l shew you a Scene indeed; or, rather, indeed, the Scene of Scenes. 'Tis an Heroic Scene."

31. For the possible implications of Scriblerus's reference to Shakespeare, see Hunter, *Occasional Form*, pp. 24–32.

32. Preface to *The Tragedy of Tragedies*, p. 45. Cf. the prologue to *The Rehearsal:* "We might well call this short Mock-play of ours / A Posie made of Weeds instead of Flowers; / Yet such have been presented to your noses, / And there are such, I fear, who thought 'em Roses." This is the gist of Fielding's reply to the critics of his play.

33. *The Tragedy of Tragedies*, p. 93.

34. For a brief account of these forty-two plays, see Hillhouse, pp. 24–36, and notes to *The Tragedy of Tragedies*.

35. As Hillhouse suggests, however, these addenda belong to the genre: "Without a preface a burlesque tragedy would hardly be complete, for the dramatist had been, since Dryden, an inveterate writer of prefaces" (p. 37). I accept this view but would add that Fielding used his scriblerian prefaces and notes to justify his motives for choosing to write a "laughing" tragedy.

CHAPTER 4

The Generous Method of the Heroic Muse:
Rape upon Rape

1. For the performance data of *Rape upon Rape*, see *The London Stage*, Part 3, 1:68 ff. *The Coffee-House Politician* was acted at the Haymarket on 30 November 1730, with *Tom Thumb* and *The Battle of the Poets* (p. 97); it was performed four times at Lincoln's Inn Fields in December 1730.

2. *Rape upon Rape*, in Henley, 9:108.

3. Justice Squeezum makes explicit the connection between attacks "against the officers of the government" like himself and "damnable conspiracies"—he recalls the "gunpowder treason plot"—"against the government" (5.6. [146]). For the Charteris background, see Goldgar, *Walpole and the Wits*, pp. 105–10; and Rogers, *Fielding: A Biography*, pp. 49–50. One contemporary pamphlet on the subject—*The Life of Colonel Don Francisco* (1730)—published after Charteris had been sentenced to death but before the pardon, deserves special attention because it emphasizes two aspects of Charteris's life that are prominent features, as my reading will show, of Fielding's play: the Colonel's "gaming" (pp. 8–9) and his attempt to "prepare" evidence (pp. 53–4).

4. Goldgar, *Walpole and the Wits*, p. 106. For instance, in the *Grub-Street Journal*, no. 10 (12 March 1730), Bavius attacks Charteris without mentioning him.

5. *Plutus*, Dedication to Lord Talbot, pp. a2f.

6. For a summary of Fielding's attitude toward Mandeville—who appears as "Mandevil" in *Amelia*—see *Tom Jones*, p. 268, n. 2.

7. Battestin, ed., *Joseph Andrews* (Middletown, Conn.: Wesleyan Univ. Press, 1967), p. 267.

8. The reference here is, of course, to Gilbert Burnet's posthu-

mously published *History of My Own Time*, 2 vols. (1723–34). Since Field-ing shared the Whig bias of the controversial latitudinarian bishop of Salisbury, he regarded him as an "impartial" historian. See *A Full Vindi-cation of the Dutchess Dowager of Marlborough* (1742). Justice Squeezum's *History*, an exercise in "the thing that is not," is emphatically "partial," both in its incompleteness and in its fictiveness.

9. In one of his explanatory notes to *Harlequin-Horace* (l. 299), James Miller also stresses the unsuitability of Charteris, his reputation notwith-standing, for committing the rape of which he was convicted: "The no-torious Colonel *Chartres*, after having, with Impunity, been guilty of diverse Misdemeanors highly worthy of the Gallows, was at last sentenc'd to it for one which he was not capable of committing; being sent to *Newgate* and condemn'd at the *Old Baily* for a *Rape*, when full *Threescore* Years old, and well-nigh *Bed-ridden* withal."

CHAPTER 5
A Master Honored and Improved:
The Grub-Street Opera and *The Beggar's Opera*

1. Cited by L. J. Morrissey in "A Note on the Text" in his edition of *The Grub-Street Opera* (Edinburgh: Oliver & Boyd, 1973), p. 14. Unless otherwise indicated, all quotations from the play are from this edition.

2. For accounts of the fortunes and misfortunes of *The Grub-Street Opera*, see Jack Richard Brown, "Henry Fielding's *Grub-Street Opera*," *Modern Language Quarterly* 16 (1955): 32–41; Hume, *Fielding and the London Theatre*, pp. 93–104; Edgar V. Roberts's Introduction to his edition of the play (Lincoln: Univ. of Nebraska Press, 1968), pp. xi–xxv; and Morris-sey's "A Note on the Text," pp. 13–24.

3. Goldgar, *Walpole and the Wits*, p. 113.

4. Morrissey makes a convincing case for this attribution. See "A Note on the Text," pp. 17–18.

5. Morrissey, "A Note on the Text," p. 16.

6. The line in quotation marks comes from a letter, probably writ-ten by Fielding, which appeared in the *Daily Post* on 28 June 1731 (Mor-rissey, "A Note on the Text," p. 14). E. Rayner, as Morrissey observes, "shared type, printers' devices and premises" with Wm. Rayner, who "is-sued some of the most seditious pamphlets and anti-government broad-sides of the time," including the Opposition journal the *Craftsman* (p. 16); the two might have been the same person. E. Rayner's publication of *The*

Welsh Opera and *The Genuine Grub-Street Opera* testifies to the plays' anti-ministerial content as well as to their usefulness as political propaganda. Fielding's discomfort was understandable. He had to dissociate himself from his work, now so closely identified with the Opposition, to keep alive his interest with the prime minister.

7. Morrissey, "A Note on the Text," pp. 19–23.

8. For information about virtually every aspect of Gay's ballad opera, see William Eben Schultz, *Gay's Beggar's Opera: Its Content, History, and Influence* (New Haven: Yale Univ. Press, 1923). See also Edgar V. Roberts's Introduction to his edition of the play (Lincoln: Univ. of Nebraska Press, 1969), pp. xii–xxviii.

9. Edmond McAdoo Gagey, *Ballad Opera* (New York: Columbia Univ. Press, 1937), p. 139.

10. The author of this piece (perhaps William Hatchett) took "Mountfort's" *King Edward III* (1691) and, as he announces in his prologue, changed "the ancient for the modern Dress" to dramatize how the "*British* Constitution . . . by *one bad Man* was almost sacrific'd." At the end of the play the king, no longer misled by the mystifications of Mortimer [Walpole], orders the execution of the "*Villain-Statesman.*" "Such be the Fate of all," the king concludes, "who dare abuse / The Ministerial Function" (p. 61). For a reading of the play, see *Fog's Weekly* (19 June 1731). Three days after *The Fall of Mortimer* was closed by "the High Constable" (*Daily Journal*, 22 July), *Fog's Weekly* (24 July), not wishing to let this particular campaign against Walpole fizzle out, fired another shot at the prime minister. Mortimer was played by Mullart, who also played the part of Robin in *The Welsh Opera;* Mullart's first role in a Fielding play had been Luckless in *The Author's Farce.*

11. Hume, *Fielding and the London Theatre*, p. 104.

12. John Loftis, *The Politics of Drama in Augustan England* (Oxford: Clarendon Press, 1963), p. 105.

13. A recent example of the perils of an exclusively political approach to the plays is Brian McCrea's chapter on Fielding's drama in his *Henry Fielding and the Politics of Mid-Eighteenth-Century England* (Athens: Univ. of Georgia Press, 1981), pp. 50–77. Because McCrea's book is so admirable in its treatment of Fielding's political motives during a life characterized by puzzling shifts in party allegiance, his failure to understand the plays is particularly disturbing. By positing a dichotomy between Fielding's regular drama (pro-Cibber, pro-Steele, pro-government) and his irregular satires (pro-scriblerian, especially pro-Gay, anti-Cibber, anti-government), McCrea arrives at a less than accurate assessment of his

"undistinguished career as a dramatist." For another study of Fielding's politics, see Thomas R. Cleary, *Henry Fielding: Political Writer* (Waterloo, Ont.: Wilfrid Laurier Univ. Press, 1984).

14. Richard Cambridge reported the story to Boswell, who recorded it in his *Life of Johnson*, p. 630 (entry for Tuesday, 18 April 1775). For other reactions to the play's opening night, see Schultz, *Gay's Beggar's Opera*, pp. 3–5. For an analysis of Gay's disconcerting double perspective, see Peter E. Lewis, "The Uncertainty Principle in *The Beggar's Opera*," *Durham University Journal* 72 (1980): 143–46.

15. A modest sampling of twentieth-century interpretations of the play may be found in Yvonne Noble, ed., *The Beggar's Opera: A Collection of Critical Essays* (Englewood Cliffs, N.J.: Prentice-Hall, 1975). See also Robert D. Hume, " 'The World is all Alike': Satire in *The Beggar's Opera*," in Hume, *The Rakish Stage*, pp. 245–69.

16. For the key to the political allegory of *The Grub-Street Opera*, see Brown (37–38), Morrissey (pp. 6–7), and Roberts (pp. xvii–xviii). I must acknowledge, in fairness to these critics, that they mention other aspects of the play; but their treatment of them is perfunctory at best. In their minds, these are obviously not so important as the political allegory and, as a result, need not be dealt with very carefully. I also realize that introductory essays, as these are, need not be comprehensive; I only point out that their emphases are decidedly political.

17. Edgar V. Roberts, ed., *The Grub-Street Opera*, pp. 77–78.

18. Even the most cursory glance at *The London Stage* for the years immediately following *The Beggar's Opera* will validate this observation. It is not unusual, therefore, to find *The Beggar's Opera* lumped together with other threats to the English dramatic tradition. Thus William Egerton, in the conclusion to his *Faithful Memoirs of the Life . . .* [of] *Mrs. Anne Oldfield* (London, 1731), writes that "the *Italian* Opera, the *Beggar*'s Opera, and other such like Farcical, and gewgau [*sic*] Pantomime Entertainments, which are of late introduced, can leave no Trace behind them that can be of Service beyond the present Moment" (p. 149).

19. Roberts, ed., *The Beggar's Opera*, p. 82.

20. Ibid. It is important to note here that, while these endings might violate certain generic expectations, they do not really contravene the expectations of *this* particular genre: improbable happy endings *belong* in an opera. See Herbert Lindenberger, *Opera: The Extravagant Art* (Ithaca, N.Y.: Cornell Univ. Press, 1984).

21. See Jeremy Collier, *A Short View of the Immorality and Profaneness of the English Stage* (London, 1698), in particular its fourth chapter, "The Stage-Poets Make Their Principal Persons Vicious and Reward Them at

the End of the Play." For two of the more vitriolic post-Collier attacks on the theater, see Arthur Bedford, *A serious Remonstrance In Behalf of the Christian Religion, against The Horrid Blasphemies and Impieties which are still used in the* English *Play-Houses* (London, 1719) and William Law, *The Absolute Unlawfulness of the Stage-Entertainment Fully Demonstrated* (London, 1726). Unlike Law, who believes that "the Business of a *Player* is prophane, wicked, lewd, and immodest" (p. 9) and therefore to be condemned and eradicated, Bedford allows that the theater *might* be morally useful; yet contemporary playwrights fail to exercise enough control on their material and thereby on their audiences: "The only Method which the *Plays* promote for a *Reformation* of Manners, is to let every Man alone, to do what he pleases, and to go on without constraint" (p. 215). For an account of the context and implications of attacks on the theater, see Jonas Barish, *The Antitheatrical Prejudice* (Berkeley and Los Angeles: Univ. of California Press, 1981); Barish deals with the Collier controversy in his eighth chapter, "Immorality and Profaneness," pp. 221–55.

22. Letter "To the Author of the London Journal" (30 March 1728), cited by Schultz, *Gay's Beggar's Opera*, p. 230. Schultz devotes a chapter to "The Morality Question"; see pp. 226–69.

23. Schultz, pp. 226–77.

24. *Mist's Weekly Journal*, no. 168 (6 July 1728), cited by Schultz, pp. 228–29. Swift's defense of *The Beggar's Opera* also addresses the issue of Italian opera; this paragraph, not cited by Schultz, suggests why Gay might have depicted his hero as such a monument to prolific heterosexuality: "This *Comedy* likewise exposeth with great Justice, that unnatural Taste for *Italian* Musick among us, which is wholly unsuitable to our Northern *Climate*, and the *Genius* of the People, whereby we are over-run with *Italian Effeminacy*, and *Italian* Nonsense. An old Gentleman said to me, that many Years ago, when the Practice of an unnatural Vice grew so frequent in *London*, that many were Prosecuted for it, he was sure it would be a forerunner of *Italian Opera's*, and Singers; and then we should want nothing but Stabbing or Poisoning, to make us perfect *Italians*."

25. Roberts, ed., *The Beggar's Opera*, p. 82.

26. Letter to the *London Journal* (30 March 1728), cited by Schultz, p. 230.

27. Schultz, pp. 231–32.

28. For documents relating John Fielding's objections to *The Beggar's Opera* and arguments for its defense, see Schultz, pp. 244–49.

29. Aristotle, *On Poetry and Style*, p. 7.

30. Battestin, ed., *Joseph Andrews*, p. 17. Cf. Dedication to *Don Quixote in England*: "It is the opinion of an author well known to your Lord-

ship [Chesterfield], that examples work quicker and stronger on the minds of men than precepts" (Henley, XI, p. 7).

31. Roberts, ed., *The Grub-Street Opera*, p. 77.

32. Morrissey, ed., *The Grub-Street Opera*, p. 28.

33. Morrissey, ed., *The Tragedy of Tragedies*, pp. 43–44.

34. Morrissey, ed., *The Grub-Street Opera*, p. 28.

35. Morrissey, ed., *The Grub-Street Opera*, p. 26.

36. *The Beggar's Opera*, p. 53.

37. Ibid., p. 55. In constructing this scene, Scriblerus may have had in mind his own mathematical method of measuring an imitation against its model. As the learned critic observes in an explanatory footnote to *The Tragedy of Tragedies* (p. 58), "*Massinissa* [in Thomson's *Sophonisba*, 3.2] is one fourth less happy than *Tom Thumb*," as indicated by the former's trimming of one "happy"—"Oh! happy, happy, happy"—from the latter's "Oh! happy, happy, happy, happy, *Thumb!*" By having Scriblerus Secundus "out-madam" Gay fifteen to nine, Fielding leaves no doubt as to his source.

38. *The Grub-Street Opera*, pp. 59–60.

39. In the introduction to *The Grub-Street Opera*, Scriblerus comments on this cornerstone of his dramatic method: "Too much altercation is the particular property of Grub-street: with what spirit do Robin and Will rap out the lie at one another for half a page together—you lie, and you lie—ah! ah! the whole wit of Grub-street consists in these two little words—you lie" (p. 27). Cf. Machine in *Tumble-Down Dick:* "He leaning against the scene is Phaeton: and the lady is Clymene. . . . This scene, sir, is in the true altercative, or scolding style of the ancients" (Henley, 12:14).

40. For Fielding's defense, in which he answers the ill-natured barbs of the *Grub-Street Journal* by impersonating a critic of scriblerian ingenuity who likes to sprinkle his discourse with Latin tags and references to "Aristuttle" and "Horase," see the prolegomena to *The Covent-Garden Tragedy* (Henley, 10:103–10). For a detailed account of Fielding's debt to Philips, see Peter Lewis, "Fielding's *The Covent-Garden Tragedy* and Philips's *The Distrest Mother*," *Durham University Journal* 37 (1975): 33–46.

41. At two crucial points in *The Grub-Street Opera*, Fielding calls attention to the seductive power of music. In the first instance, Master Owen, having reached the limits of his eloquence in his argument for heeding "natural" desires, resorts to two songs (nos. 25 and 26) to convince Molly that they can be "married" without a "parson" (pp. 51–52). In the second instance, at the end of the play, Master Owen encourages

Molly to try the same strategy on his father when he tells her to "ply him with songs till he forgives us" (p. 83) for marrying without his consent.

42. *The Beggar's Opera*, p. 83.

CHAPTER 6

The Mimesis of Morality: *The Modern Husband*

1. Cross, *History of Henry Fielding*, 1:117.

2. Prologue to *The Lottery*, in Henley, 8:267.

3. Cross, *History of Henry Fielding*, 1:116–17. See also Edgar V. Roberts, "Fielding's Ballad Opera *The Lottery* (1732) and the English State Lottery of 1731," *Huntington Library Quarterly* 27 (1963): 39–52.

4. I am here adapting Fielding's famous epithet for *Amelia* in the *Covent-Garden Journal* (25 January 1752).

5. Robert Halsband, ed., *The Complete Letters of Lady Mary Wortley Montagu* (Oxford: Clarendon Press, 1966), 2:93.

6. Cross, *History of Henry Fielding*, 1:121. In *A Complete History of the Stage*, 5 vols. (London, 1800), Charles Dibdin remarks that "*The Modern Husband* . . . was a sound written comedy, but it was not sufficiently ballanced by either pleasantry or interest" (5:41). John Genest is even less enthusiastic: "The characters of Mr. and Mrs. Modern are well conceived, but this Comedy is on the whole a dull piece of business" (*Some Account of the English Stage from the Restoration in 1660 to 1830*, 10 vols. [Bath, 1832], 3:332). Even Hume, whose account of the piece is largely sympathetic, concludes that "Fielding's reiterated partiality for this play is no credit to his judgment" (*Fielding and the London Theatre*, p. 128).

7. *Grub-Street Journal*, no. 117 (30 March 1732), reprinted in Ronald Paulson and Thomas Lockwood, ed., *Henry Fielding: The Critical Heritage* (London: Routledge and Kegan Paul, 1969), p. 31. For Fielding's quarrel with the *Grub-Street Journal*—a quarrel that may have been politically motivated—see Cross, *History of Henry Fielding*, pp. 114–41; with the exception of Fielding's prolegomena to *The Covent-Garden Tragedy*, the most important documents in this lengthy and tedious squabble are reprinted by Paulson and Lockwood, pp. 30–67. Since virtually every modern critic of *The Modern Husband* has commented extensively on this quarrel and on the other political implications of the piece—most notably whether Fielding's dedication to Walpole must be taken at face value (Loftis, p. 130; Goldgar, *Walpole and the Wits*, pp. 112–13) or ironically (Hunter, pp. 56–57)—I have decided to break precedent and analyze the play itself.

8. *Letters of Lady Mary Wortley Montagu*, p. 93. It must be emphasized here that this was a model which *Fielding* himself had not attempted. He would have been aware that marital conflict had been the subject of many Restoration and eighteenth-century plays; the Vanbrugh-Cibber opposition I refer to in my opening chapter, for example, centered around the faithful representation of the subject, with *The Provok'd Husband* being the most prominent recent example of this dramatic type. Fielding, however, is correct in claiming originality; no other play on the subject exhibits the unrelenting nastiness of *The Modern Husband*.

9. In *Fielding: A Biography*, for example, Rogers writes: "I am bound to confess . . . that I would rather attend a second-rate performance of *The Lottery* than endure the five-act virtue-in-distress which constitutes *The Modern Husband*" (p. 54). F. W. Bateson, who has little respect for Fielding's dramatic abilities, dismisses the play with a terse fulmination worthy of the *Grub-Street Journal*: "*The Modern Husband* must be one of the dullest productions ever fathered by a man of genius" (*English Comic Drama, 1700–1750* [Oxford: Oxford Univ. Press, 1929], pp. 115–16). Bateson is, of course, wrong: that dubious distinction belongs to *The Universal Gallant* (1735), Fielding's last regular comedy before 1737.

10. For a discussion of this law, see Charles B. Woods, "Notes on Three of Fielding's Plays," *PMLA* 52 (1937): 359–73. See also Robert D. Hume, "Marital Discord in English Comedy from Dryden to Fielding," *Modern Philology* 75 (1977): 248–72. In a case of life imitating art which would have delighted Oscar Wilde, Theophilus Cibber, who played the part of Captain Bellamant, attempted to take advantage of this "wholesome law," but, as usual with the lesser Cibber, his plot misfired. As the author of *The Comforts of Matrimony; Exemplified in the Memorable Case and Trial, Lately had Upon an ACTION brought by Theo——s C——r against — — S——, Esq; for Criminal Conversation with the Plaintiff's Wife* (London, 1739) observes: "'The Lord Chief Justice then summ'd up the Evidence on both Sides, and directed the Jury to bring in their Verdict, which, after a short Stay, they did, and found for the Plaintiff TEN POUNDS Damages" (p. 37). Cibber had asked for two thousand pounds (p. 20).

11. For the reaction of Dramaticus to Fielding's "monsters," see the *Grub-Street Journal* (30 March 1732), in *Henry Fielding: The Critical Heritage*, p. 36.

12. For John Loftis's comments on *The Modern Husband*, see Loftis, Richard Southern, Marion Jones, and A. H. Scouten, ed., *The Revels History of Drama in English* (London: Methuen, 1976), 5:72–73.

13. Cross, *History of Henry Fielding*, 1:119.

14. Fielding might have borrowed the card game as controlling im-

age from Congreve's *The Way of the World* (1700), which opens with Mirabell and Fainall "rising from cards."

15. The beginning of *The Modern Husband* recalls the opening scene (ll. 36–79) of "The Journal of a Modern Lady" (1729); the poem, attributed to Pope and Swift, was reprinted in the 1732 edition of Richard Seymour's *The Court Gamester;* a section of this popular work deals with picquet, its rules, and hints toward the detection of cheats.

16. This is also the predicament of Lady Townly in the fifth act of Cibber's *The Provok'd Husband*. In a "Dressing Room" scene which could well have been the model of Fielding's own scene here, Lady Townly confides to her maid Trusty that she "want[s] Money infinitely oftener than [her husband] is willing to give it."

17. W. B. Carnochan, ed., *Sir Fopling Flutter: or, The Man of Mode* (Lincoln: Univ. of Nebraska Press, 1966), p. 23.

18. For the story of these years, see Hume, *Fielding and the London Theatre*, pp. 129–99.

19. For an analysis of this play, see the article by Peter Lewis cited above (chapter 5, n. 40). Fielding might have taken a hint for his title from a couplet in Steele's fulsome prologue to *The Distrest Mother:* "'Tis nothing, when a fancy'd Scene's in View, / To skip from *Covent-Garden* to *Peru*" (ll. 7–8). I quote these lines from the 1735 London edition of the play.

20. See Charles B. Woods, "Cibber in Fielding's *Author's Farce:* Three Notes," *Philological Quarterly* 44 (1965): 145–51. For discussions of the political implications of literary references to Colley Cibber, see Maynard Mack, *The Garden and the City: Retirement and Politics in the Later Poetry of Pope, 1731–1743* (Toronto: Toronto Univ. Press, 1969), esp. pp. 157–62; and Aubrey L. Williams, *Pope's Dunciad: A Study of Its Meaning* (London: Methuen, 1955). For Theophilus Cibber's version of the actors' revolt, see *Theophilus Cibber, to David Garrick, Esq; with Dissertations on Theatrical Subjects* (London, 1759), pp. 19–21.

21. Preface to *Don Quixote in England*, in Henley, 11:9.

22. On this point, see Introduction, n. 9, above.

CHAPTER 7

The Politics of the Playhouse:
Pasquin and *The Historical Register for the Year 1736*

1. William W. Appleton, ed., *The Historical Register for the Year 1736 and Eurydice Hiss'd* (Lincoln: Univ. of Nebraska Press, 1967), p. 13.

2. Ibid., p. 16. On the meaning of "farce" and the correspondences

between stage and state in Fielding's plays, see Ronald Paulson, *Satire and the Novel in Eighteenth-Century England* (New Haven: Yale Univ. Press, 1967), pp. 85–95. For an excellent discussion of Fielding's strategies in his last "reflexive plays," see Hunter, *Occasional Form*, pp. 49–74.

3. In *The Egoist: or, Colley upon Cibber* (London, 1743) Cibber, while pointedly refusing to name his antagonist, records his "good-natured" reaction to Fielding's attack: "Don't you remember, at the little Theatre in the *Hay-Market*, upon the first Day of acting some new Piece there? when a personal Jest upon me flew souce in my Face, while I sat in the Eye of a full Audience, was not I as suddenly loud in my Laugh and Applause, as any common Spectator? Now as I could have no Warning of the Shot, was not my manner of receiving it a plain Proof that I was more pleased with the Conceit, than hurt with the Intention of it?" (pp. 27–28). This little pamphlet is also remarkable in revealing that Cibber, after having "been so used to play[ing] the Fool in Comedy," had begun "to be quite as easy, in the same Character, in real Life" (p. 35): "Why, how do you think I could have given you so finish'd a Coxcomb [Lord Foppington] if I had not found a good deal of the same Stuff in myself to make him with?" (p. 38).

4. O. M. Brack, Jr., William Kupersmith, and Curt A. Zimansky, eds., *Pasquin* (Iowa City: Univ. of Iowa Press, 1973), p. 37.

5. For the stage history of *Pasquin*, see the Introduction by Brack et al., pp. vii–xviii; and Hume, *Fielding and the London Theatre*, pp. 209–20.

6. Cited from facsimile of original title page, in *Pasquin*, p. 1.

7. See the *Grub-Street Journal*, no. 330 (22 April 1736) and no. 332 (6 May 1736). Marforio here offers an uninspired rebuttal to what was perhaps the most interesting contemporary analysis (in terms of painting) of the play's dramatic method, Aaron Hill's commendatory essay in *The Prompter* (2 April 1736). These three pieces, together with other contemporary documents dealing with *Pasquin* and *The Historical Register*, are reprinted in *Henry Fielding: The Critical Heritage*, pp. 77–110.

8. See the *Champion* (19 August 1740). Cf. *Tom Jones*, 7.1 "A Comparison between the World and the Stage."

9. Goldgar, *Walpole and the Wits*, p. 151. Goldgar is here speaking of all of Fielding's plays from *Don Quixote in England* to *Eurydice Hiss'd*: "Nor are the plays . . . heavily or bitterly satiric, not at least when compared to other political satires of the time. Fielding's persistent themes, aside from the perennial topic of corruption, are political motifs which have the maximum *literary* significance: that is, he is acutely sensitive to the triumph of the 'sons of dullness' over men of wit and merit and to

efforts to limit the freedom of the stage." I agree with Goldgar, but would add that few of Fielding's patrons at the Haymarket would have failed to notice that the vast majority of the "sons of dullness" seemed to belong to Walpole's camp; moreover, *The Historical Register*, though it may not have been "heavily or bitterly satiric" in performance, becomes downright offensive when read after Fielding's Dedication to the Public.

10. In 1729, for example, Walpole had revived the old statute and suppressed Gay's *Polly*. Although the Licensing Act provides the catastrophe for Fielding's dramatic career, its story does not really belong in a critical study of his plays. For the definitive study of the subject, see Vincent J. Liesenfeld, *The Licensing Act of 1737* (Madison: Univ. of Wisconsin Press, 1984). On Fielding and the Licensing Act, see Hume, *Fielding and the London Theatre*, pp. 248–53.

11. Biblical quotations are from the King James Version; those of *Paradise Lost* from Merritt Y. Hughes, ed., *John Milton: Complete Poems and Major Prose* (New York: Odyssey, 1957).

12. See Charles W. Nichols, "Social Satire in *Pasquin* and *The Historical Register*," *Philological Quarterly* 3 (1924): 309–17. On Fielding's fun at the Cibbers' expense, see, in addition to the sources already cited, Charles W. Nichols, "Fielding and the Cibbers," *Philological Quarterly* 1 (1922): 278–89; and Houghton W. Taylor, "Fielding upon Cibber," *Modern Philology* 29 (1931): 73–90.

13. The *Craftsmen*, no. 403 (23 March 1734) offers a discussion of the popular stage-state term *screen:* "A *Screen* in the metaphorical Sense, means any Device, or Contrivance, to protect Men from the Fury of their Enemies, or the Pursuit of Justice. . . . Hence it appears, *Screening* is absolutely necessary, when *publick Corruption grows prevalent;* and in whom can this great Privilege be so properly reposed, as in a *Prime Minister,* who conducts the whole Machine of Government, and is therefore the best Judge who are the proper Objects of Favour." This piece is attributed to Fielding in Martin C. Battestin's forthcoming *New Essays by Henry Fielding* (University Press of Virginia).

14. For the stage history of *The Historical Register* and *Eurydice Hiss'd*, see Appleton's introduction, pp. xii–xviii.

15. Ibid., p. xiii. Appleton cites other relevant entries from Egmont's diary on p. xii.

16. On the last days of the Great Mogul's Company—including Fielding's scheme for building a new theatre as well as the tantalizing probability that, at the end, Fielding was bought off by Walpole—see Hume, *Fielding and the London Theatre*, pp. 239–53.

Index